Thucydides: A Very Short Introduction

VERY SHORT INTRODUCTIONS are for anyone wanting a stimulating and accessible way into a new subject. They are written by experts, and have been translated into more than 45 different languages.

The series began in 1995, and now covers a wide variety of topics in every discipline. The VSI library currently contains over 750 volumes—a Very Short Introduction to everything from Psychology and Philosophy of Science to American History and Relativity—and continues to grow in every subject area.

Very Short Introductions available now:

ABOLITIONISM Richard S. Newman
THE ABRAHAMIC RELIGIONS
   Charles L. Cohen
ACCOUNTING Christopher Nobes
ADDICTION Keith Humphreys
ADOLESCENCE Peter K. Smith
THEODOR W. ADORNO
   Andrew Bowie
ADVERTISING Winston Fletcher
AERIAL WARFARE Frank Ledwidge
AESTHETICS Bence Nanay
AFRICAN AMERICAN HISTORY
   Jonathan Scott Holloway
AFRICAN AMERICAN RELIGION
   Eddie S. Glaude Jr.
AFRICAN HISTORY John Parker
   and Richard Rathbone
AFRICAN POLITICS Ian Taylor
AFRICAN RELIGIONS Jacob K. Olupona
AGEING Nancy A. Pachana
AGNOSTICISM Robin Le Poidevin
AGRICULTURE Paul Brassley and
   Richard Soffe
ALEXANDER THE GREAT
   Hugh Bowden
ALGEBRA Peter M. Higgins
AMERICAN BUSINESS HISTORY
   Walter A. Friedman
AMERICAN CULTURAL HISTORY
   Eric Avila
AMERICAN FOREIGN RELATIONS
   Andrew Preston
AMERICAN HISTORY Paul S. Boyer

AMERICAN IMMIGRATION
   David A. Gerber
AMERICAN INTELLECTUAL
   HISTORY
   Jennifer Ratner-Rosenhagen
THE AMERICAN JUDICIAL SYSTEM
   Charles L. Zelden
AMERICAN LEGAL HISTORY
   G. Edward White
AMERICAN MILITARY HISTORY
   Joseph T. Glatthaar
AMERICAN NAVAL HISTORY
   Craig L. Symonds
AMERICAN POETRY David Caplan
AMERICAN POLITICAL HISTORY
   Donald Critchlow
AMERICAN POLITICAL PARTIES
   AND ELECTIONS L. Sandy Maisel
AMERICAN POLITICS
   Richard M. Valelly
THE AMERICAN PRESIDENCY
   Charles O. Jones
THE AMERICAN REVOLUTION
   Robert J. Allison
AMERICAN SLAVERY
   Heather Andrea Williams
THE AMERICAN SOUTH
   Charles Reagan Wilson
THE AMERICAN WEST Stephen Aron
AMERICAN WOMEN'S HISTORY
   Susan Ware
AMPHIBIANS T. S. Kemp
ANAESTHESIA Aidan O'Donnell

Available soon:

For more information visit our website

www.oup.com/vsi/

Jennifer T. Roberts

THUCYDIDES

A Very Short Introduction

OXFORD
UNIVERSITY PRESS

Great Clarendon Street, Oxford, OX2 6DP,
United Kingdom

Oxford University Press is a department of the University of Oxford.
It furthers the University's objective of excellence in research, scholarship,
and education by publishing worldwide. Oxford is a registered trade mark of
Oxford University Press in the UK and in certain other countries

© Jennifer T. Roberts 2024

The moral rights of the author have been asserted

Published in the United States of America by Oxford University Press
198 Madison Avenue, New York, NY 10016, United States of America

British Library Cataloguing in Publication Data

Data available

Library of Congress Control Number: 2024937963

ISBN 978–0–19–285582–4

Printed and bound by
CPI Group (UK) Ltd, Croydon, CR0 4YY

Links to third party websites are provided by Oxford in good faith and
for information only. Oxford disclaims any responsibility for the materials
contained in any third party website referenced in this work.

The manufacturer's authorised representative in the EU for product safety is Oxford
University Press España S.A. of el Parque Empresarial San Fernando de Henares,
Avenida de Castilla, 2 – 28830 Madrid (www.oup.es/en).

for Walter Blanco,
who heard Thucydides' voice like no other

Contents

Timeline

All translations from the Greek are my own.
All dates are BCE unless otherwise specified.

List of illustrations

Chapter 1
The world of Thucydides

Why does life proceed as it does? What explains the fact that things turn out as they do rather than in some other way? Human foresight—or the lack of it? Divine oversight? Fate? Chance? We all ask these questions; those of us who become historians are forced to grapple with them on a regular basis, and historians have been at work for a very long time.

In the year we know today as 424 BCE, when Athens and Sparta had been at war for seven years, the dynamic Spartan general Brasidas moved on the cities in the northern reaches of the Athenian Empire with astonishing speed. Marching through the long December night and undeterred by falling snow, he persuaded the citizens of the strategically located Athenian colony of Amphipolis (Figure 1) to abandon their allegiance to Athens and come over to Sparta. The defection of Amphipolis would have a profound effect not only on the course of the war but on the way that war's history would be written. For the irate Athenians responded by exiling the young general they had put in charge in the region: Thucydides, son of Olorus. 'It came about', Thucydides wrote, 'that I was banished from my country for 20 years after my command at Amphipolis, and being able to interact with both sides (not least the Spartans and their allies because of my exile), I had the opportunity to scrutinize developments without distraction.'

1

BLACK SEA

MACEDONIA

Epidamnus

THRACE

Pella   Amphipolis

Thasos

Corcyra

Lesbos

Delphi

Thebes   LYDIA

Corinth Megara

Athens Ephesus   ANATOLIA

MESSENIA   Miletus

Sparta

LACONIA

Cos

Rhodes

Crete   Cyprus

*MEDITERRANEAN
SEA*

Cyrene •

EGYPT

Nile River

0	100	200		300 miles
0	100	200	300 400	500 km

1. Map of mainland Greece.

Because Sparta and most of its allies were located in the large peninsula of the Peloponnesus in mainland Greece, the war they fought with Athens is usually known today as the Peloponnesian War, although the Spartans no doubt called it the Athenian War

2

and Thucydides refers to it as 'the war of the Peloponnesians and Athenians'. The account Thucydides gave of the war was a highly individual one, shaped to convey its author's sense of what the long years of fighting had to teach us about the subject that interested him above all else: human nature. In Thucydides' *History* (as I will call it, though the author gave it no name), we hear the anguished cries of a man who saw the world he had known passing away as Greek sensibilities hardened before his eyes. As the fighting wears on, the Athenians become increasingly comfortable killing and enslaving non-combatants; the Spartans abandon their fair promises to liberate the Greeks and instead sell them out to Persia in exchange for contributions to their war chest; vicious civil wars erupt across the Greek world; mercenaries break into a school and butcher all the children.

The war played a pivotal role in Greek history. It brought the Athenian Empire to an end; it embroiled Persia in Greek affairs; it positioned Sparta to dominate Greece during the decades that followed its defeat of Athens; and it put an end to any hope that the Greek states might unify in such a way as to hold off the threat that would develop in the north as Philip of Macedon made it his mission to absorb the Greek mainland into his domains. It also provided the subject matter for the comedies of Aristophanes and exacerbated hostility to the provocative intellectual Socrates. Socrates' execution in turn put the capstone on Plato's alienation from democracy, a development that propelled him to formulate a philosophy whose influence on the history of thought is incalculable. Most of all, it produced unspeakable suffering. As Thucydides wrote,

> this war was of protracted duration and inflicted such misery on Greece as had never before been known in such a period of time. Never before had so many cities been captured and emptied of their inhabitants, sometimes by foreigners, sometimes by Greeks warring with one another, the former populace being sometimes removed to make room for new settlers. Never before had there been so much exiling and so much killing.

The significance of Thucydides' work was immediately recognized; much copied, it was read by a number of educated people throughout the Greek world and in time by Romans as well. None of these early versions survives, but the text was preserved in seven medieval manuscripts, the earliest complete one dated to around 900 CE and the earliest fragments to around 300 CE. The manuscripts can be found today in Paris, in the Vatican, in Florence, in London, in Munich (two), and in Heidelberg, and Thucydides' text is now widely available throughout the world, translated into many languages.

A wealthy Athenian aristocrat, Thucydides lived during an extraordinary period in history. Although the date of his birth is uncertain—we know almost nothing about his life—he plainly reached his 30th birthday no later than 424, the year in which he was elected one of Athens's 10 generals (who also served as admirals), a position for which 30 was the minimum age. Membership in the Board of Ten was the highest honour in the state. Elected for one-year terms, but often re-elected, these men had the privilege of speaking first, in order of age, in the frequent meetings of the (male) citizens' assembly. Thucydides grew up when Athens was at the height of its power and enjoying an extraordinary cultural florescence. The tragedians Aeschylus, Sophocles, and Euripides were all presenting plays at the annual festivals in honour of the god Dionysus, along with the comic dramatist Aristophanes, who drew belly laughs as he skewered Athens's politicians. The assembly debated passionately at its outdoor meeting place. Juries composed of hundreds of men met frequently to decide a wide variety of cases, and policy was guided by the judicious statesman Pericles, regularly re-elected to the board of generals.

Athens was a cosmopolitan city that attracted many visitors. Some, like the proto-scientists Anaxagoras and Democritus, brought with them their own teachings, while others reported the researches of men like the physician Hippocrates from Cos off the coast of Anatolia. Some came to trade and left, while others came to trade and stayed. Still others came to spread their ideas in a bustling metropolis. Thucydides thus was the beneficiary not only of the rich culture of Athens but the manifold currents at work in the wider Greek world as well.

Among the most famous were the men known to history as the Sophists, itinerant intellectuals who filled the gap left in Greek education by its conspicuously literary bent, teaching young men (whose fathers could afford to pay) to question established norms and instructing them in the arts of clever argumentation. In Athens as in most of Greece, boys and the occasional girl spent most of their time memorizing and dissecting poetry, chiefly Homer, the foundational text of Greek civilization; thus Thucydides' formal education was almost entirely in verse. Along with the natural sciences, basic training in composition and argumentation was sorely lacking, as was what we would call Social Studies (a discipline that did not in fact catch on until the 19th century in Britain and the 20th elsewhere). The papers regularly written by adolescents today arguing for some position chosen by either student or teacher played no part in Greek schooling, nor did the fundamental information about the world that would have facilitated the making of such arguments. In democratic Athens, the Sophists, eager to teach about the world and how to get by in it, found a niche market. Citizens could hardly hope to persuade an audience in a courtroom or assembly meeting by quoting mellifluous passages from Homer. Into this world stepped the Sophists, eager to share their ideas about right and wrong, truth and falsehood, the gods, the laws, and much else—and, for a fee, to instruct the youth of Athens in the arts of rhetoric.

Some found their ideas new and shocking, but the Sophists could not have achieved the success they did had they not found eminently receptive audiences curious to hear people say things out loud they had been thinking for some time. (How can people really know anything about the gods, or even be sure they exist?

5

I've never seen one. What do we mean by hot or cold? Yesterday when we were walking out to the farm my son said it was chilly out, but I thought it was uncomfortably warm.) Some people were appalled when Protagoras came from Abdera in northern Greece, befriended Pericles, and announced publicly that he couldn't be sure the gods existed—it was an awfully hard question, after all—but others suspected he was on to something, and his contention that 'each individual person is the measure of all things: of things that are, that they are, and of things that are not, that they are not' also must have struck a responsive chord. Inevitably, there were those whom self-interest prompted to grab hold of dangerous ideas like the notion that laws were not god given but rather made by fallible mortals and thus might reasonably be broken. It was a question that had been tossed around for some time. Often blamed for destabilizing old and comfortable value systems, the Sophists were by no means alone in raising the kinds of questions with which any mature and complex society must grapple, and the relationship of *nomos*, custom/law (it meant both in Greek), to *physis*, nature, was widely debated in the 5th century and into the 4th. Is justice immutably grounded in nature, or is it simply a matter of obeying the laws—which, after all, sometimes change? If the latter, how is it that laws vary from one society to another? These questions went to the root of moral relativism, and then, as now, moral relativism made many people uncomfortable.

Herodotus, the magnificent historian of the Persian Wars, included in his *Histories* a tale designed to demonstrate that it is decidedly *nomos* that dominates. When Darius was king in Persia, he wrote, he gathered together some Greeks who happened to be at his court and asked of them how much money it would take to persuade them to eat the dead bodies of their fathers. The horrified Greeks replied that they would never do such a thing for any amount of money. Darius next summoned some Indians who were in the habit of doing just that and asked them, in front of the Greeks, what it would take to persuade them to allow their

6

parents to be cremated. The Indians were similarly scandalized. 'We see from this', Herodotus observed, 'how deeply rooted a thing custom is': two different cultures, two different and opposite ways of doing things. One of Herodotus' purposes in writing the *Histories* was in fact to show the Greeks that their way of life was not the only one possible. Around the same time as Herodotus was at work, the Athenian tragedian Sophocles produced his *Antigone*, a play that touches so many nerves that it has made its protagonist the poster child for civil disobedience ever since. Forbidden by her Uncle Creon, the king of Thebes, to bury her brother on the grounds that he was a traitor, she chooses death over obeying Creon's edict. After all, she explains, Creon's decree did not come from Zeus; it is not in accord with the *nomoi* that Justice has established among mortals. No mortal can override the unwritten laws laid down by the gods.

Athens in Thucydides' day was one of well over a thousand Greek cities in the classical world, a time when there was no country named Greece but rather hundreds of independent city-states or *poleis* (singular, *polis*) with populations ranging from a couple of hundred to perhaps a third of a million. Athens was by far the largest. Greek settlement extended as far north as Ukraine and as far south as Egypt, as far west as Spain and as far east as Turkey, the ancient Anatolia; Herodotus was born on the Anatolian coast in the largely Greek city of Halicarnassus, now Bodrum. During the 7th and 6th centuries, strongmen known as *tyrannoi* (hence the English word tyrant) seized power in a number of Greek states, and Athens was no exception, but by 500 tyranny had died out except in the Greek settlements in Sicily. The governments of the Greek *poleis* ranged for the most part from oligarchies of varying narrowness to what the Greeks called *demokratia*. Some states went back and forth from the one to the other, a change usually accompanied by bloodshed.

Although 'democracy' is probably the best translation and certainly the most common one, Greek *demokratia* was very different from modern democracies. No Greek state allowed women to participate in government, and all Greek states included large numbers of enslaved people, who had no say at all in the running of the state and few rights of any kind. Even in Athens, where they were welcomed for the contributions they made to the economy, immigrants and their descendants were almost never awarded citizenship. No state, however, was as inhospitable as xenophobic Sparta, which practised regular expulsions of visitors from other parts of Greece. Sparta indeed was an outlier in many respects, governed as it was by two kings concurrently—a holdover from the days when all the Greek communities were led by some 'head man'—in concert with five magistrates, a council of elders, and an assembly.

All Greek states included significant numbers of enslaved people who lacked civic rights, but Sparta was unusual in the number of its slaves: at the beginning of the 5th century the historian Herodotus numbered the slave/citizen ratio at seven to one. Though assigned to individuals, moreover, slaves in Sparta, known as helots, were in fact the property of the state. The threat posed by such a large slave population played a large role in shaping Sparta's cautious foreign policy, as Spartans were hesitant to involve themselves in long campaigns far from home, endeavours that would leave an understandably restive work force unattended. Their fears intensified after an earthquake in 464 sparked a major helot rebellion.

Not long before Thucydides' birth, Athens and Sparta joined with about 30 other Greek states to defend their civilization from the invading Persian Empire in the war that became the organizing principle of Herodotus' *Histories*, a wide-ranging project that was really an account of the many cultures that made up the world Herodotus knew. The invasion sparked terror in a people who were so fiercely independent that despite shared language, religion, and customs they had persisted for centuries in living in small autonomous communities, each with limited natural resources, rather than uniting in a single state. Nobody had been more surprised than the Greeks themselves when a badly outnumbered coalition of Athenians, flanked by men from little Plataea to their north, trounced the Persians decisively on the plain of Marathon in 490. The exasperated Persian king Darius immediately began planning a do-over, a campaign that his son and successor Xerxes inherited upon his father's death in 486.

The Persians' famous stand-off at the Thermopylae pass in central Greece with the 300 Spartans (and a number of others ignored in the historical record) ended in death for the defenders when an unguarded path was betrayed to Xerxes, but the holding operation bought time for the Greeks to the south. There, off the island of Salamis, the Greek fleet, composed of the fast, sleek ships known as triremes from their three banks of oars, defeated the invaders thanks in large part to Athenian naval expertise and the foresight of the Athenian admiral Themistocles; a land battle at Plataea the following summer ended the Persian threat once and for all. The Greeks, however, had a reasonable expectation that the Persians might try for round three, and they soon organized into a naval league to forestall this eventuality. When the Greeks received word that the Spartan commander Pausanias was behaving badly in Byzantium, parading around like an eastern potentate and generally conducting himself in an arrogant and overbearing manner—rumours the Athenians no doubt took the lead in spreading—they turned to Athens for leadership instead. Although Spartan infantry were famed for their grit, events at Salamis had shown the importance of naval power. There Athens excelled, and plainly the task of keeping the Persians at bay would call for skilled sailors, not doughty infantry.

Sparta had been for generations the most formidable power in the Greek world, and it was predictable that not all Spartans would take the meteoric rise of Athens with good grace. The Greek world was now divided into two camps. Sparta continued to head the long-standing Peloponnesian League, an organization consisting mostly of states in the peninsula of the Peloponnesus in southern Greece but benefiting from some outside it. Athens meanwhile led a new far-flung naval organization called by moderns the Delian League because of the location of the league treasury on the Aegean island of Delos; the Greeks just called it 'the Athenians and their allies'. *Allies* was a rather misleading word. From a voluntary alliance, designed to ward off future Persian attacks and wreak vengeance for the harm done to the Greeks in the war, the league soon came to be managed with an iron hand by the Athenians for their own strategic and economic benefit. From 454, when the Athenians relocated the league treasury from the Aegean island of Delos to Athens itself for purported safekeeping, historians generally refer to the league as the Athenian Empire. Far smaller and more ethnically homogeneous than other ancient empires, it has sometimes prompted historians to seek other names for it, but none seems to me to describe it as accurately as 'empire'. Though not as wealthy as the empires of Persia or, in later times, Rome, it nonetheless required a substantial treasury, and league members had the option of funding its operations by contributions of ships or money. Most opted for money.

One leading Spartan ally was Corinth, situated on the isthmus that joined the peninsula of the Peloponnesus to mainland Greece. With ports on either side of the narrow neck of land, the Corinthians traded widely and were thus natural rivals of the Athenians. Another was Thebes in the territory of Boeotia adjoining the Athenians' territory of Attica to the north, technically outside the Peloponnesus but still tightly bound to Sparta in its diplomatic history; the Thebans' magnificent soldiery was vital to the strength of the Peloponnesian League. The Athenians for their part enjoyed hegemony over a wide range of islands throughout the Aegean Sea and the coast of Anatolia, and no fleet the Spartans could put in the water was a match for their imperial navy. While the Athenians made decisions for their entire empire, both Sparta and its allies framed the foreign policy of the Peloponnesian League, and Corinth in particular would play a large role in the league's decision to go to war with Athens.

It was this bipolar world into which Thucydides was born around 454. His father's name, Olorus, links him to Thracian royalty. The daughter of an earlier Olorus, king of Thrace, had married Miltiades, the hero of Marathon and father of the pro-Spartan, anti-democratic politician Cimon. Though Thucydides' family connections were with the conservative Cimon, who had taken the lead in Athens's post-war military operations, he was nonetheless captivated by Cimon's rival, the anti-Spartan Pericles, leader of the democrats. Although just as blue-blooded as the family of Cimon and Miltiades (and Thucydides), Pericles was firmly committed to further progression in the direction of democracy in Athens, where it had been evolving for generations and would continue to evolve further. It was at Pericles' instigation that jury pay was introduced at Athens, thus ensuring that cases would be judged by a wide spectrum of (male) citizens.

Pericles was also a committed imperialist, and with the tribute paid by each subject/ally into the league treasury the ambitious building project sprang up that transformed the Athenian Acropolis into a splendid site that attracts visitors still today; the temple to Athens's tutelary goddess Athena Parthenos (Athena the Maiden) known as the Parthenon is one of the most instantly recognizable buildings in the world. When Thucydides was born there was no Parthenon; by the time he began writing his *History*, there was. In addition to proclaiming the glory of Athens, the numerous buildings that formed part of Pericles' plan for the Acropolis created countless jobs for Athens's less affluent residents.

Inevitably, objections to this use of allied funds were raised both outside Athens and within, but Pericles was a remarkable orator, and he managed to carry the people with him—at least those who were Athenian. No doubt the subject/allies remained distressed.

The position Pericles held in Athens was no different from the one to which Thucydides was elected in 424: each served as one of the 10 generals elected annually to one-year terms to command the city's armed forces on both land and sea. But because of his impressive intellect and extraordinary powers of persuasion, Pericles was re-elected virtually every year for 30 years and was still in office when he died. His enormous popularity, combined with Thucydides' dislike of democracy, led Thucydides to claim that Athens in the time of Pericles, while in name a democracy, in reality became government by the foremost citizen. He was mistaken. The highest authority in the Athenian state was not the 10 generals and certainly not a single one of them. Sovereignty lay rather with the assembly of adult male citizens, meeting several times a month. In 430, when the war was going badly, the Athenian assembly, citing some irregularities in his accounts but plainly frustrated with his conduct of the war, impeached Pericles, fined him, and removed him from office. Nothing could reveal more plainly that Athens was, in fact, the rule of the (male, adult) citizenry.

The intense involvement of Athenians with their government was magnified by the custom of choosing officials by lottery, guaranteeing that a very high proportion of citizen men had held some office or other by the time they died. Business for the assembly was prepared by a Council of Five Hundred, men chosen by lot who could initially serve only once in their lives; at some point it became possible to serve twice. Originally the nine officials known as archons, who early in Athens's history had replaced the king, were elected from prominent families, but the Persian Wars made clear that the 10 generals were more important to the well-being of the state, and in 487 the Athenians began choosing the archons by lot, thus greatly diluting the importance and prestige of the office. The size of Athens's juries combined with the Athenians' notorious litigiousness to make jury service a part of daily life for Athenian men. The lottery came into play here as well, for, to prevent bribery, nobody knew until the day of the trial on which jury he would serve.

A wider group participated eagerly in the civic life of the community. Festivals of one kind or another were held every other day or so. Because there was much food and wine on offer, people were eager to participate. The grand Panathenaea celebrating Athena was held every four years. The Dionysia honouring Dionysus provided the setting in which the tragedies and comedies for which Athens is famous were performed. Beginning with a rowdy parade in the god's honour, the festival also included singing competitions, an extravagant sacrifice of bulls, and ceremonies highlighting Athenian power, power won by military might. The generals paraded across the stage, as did boys whose fathers had been killed in battle—and there was a pointed laying out of the enforced contributions supplied by the subject allies. The message was clear: this entertainment, this food, this wine, has been provided to you by glorious Athens, to which the entire Aegean pays tribute. Isn't it all worth it?

It was this Athens that entered upon a ruinous war in the expectation that it could be easily won, this Athens whose downfall Thucydides chronicles in his *History*. In fact, great days still lay ahead for Athens after the Peloponnesian War. It was in Athens after all that Plato wrote his dialogues and founded his Academy—the Academy at which his star pupil Aristotle spent many years of his life. But Thucydides was dead by this time, and what he saw was a city devastated by war. This devastation formed his subject matter—this and much, much more. Knowing that his readers were accustomed to the charms of mythology, the derring-do of the *Iliad*, the fantastic escapades of the *Odyssey*, the lively and often amusing tales of Herodotus, and sophistic displays full of purple passages, Thucydides expresses concern that the absence of what he calls *to muthodes* from his *History* may put readers off. Some people, he cautions us,

> may find my narrative less pleasing because it lacks *to muthodes*
> (the mythical, the fictional, the romantic). Those, however, who
> want to see things exactly as they were as an aid to understanding

the future, which, human nature being what it is, will resemble the past, may deem this work useful. I have written this book not as a composition to win the applause of the moment but as a possession for all time.

It is not unusual for authors to promise readers a good time at the outset of their books. You are really going to enjoy this, they assure us in what is known by the Latin term *captatio benevolentiae*, the capturing of good will. Thucydides takes a conspicuously opposite tack. If you're expecting a good time, he warns us, you may be sadly disappointed. Fair warning: no fun to be had here. If, on the other hand, you are a better human being than that; if you are one of those who is really interested in getting at the truth—well, in that case, you are my kind of person. Read on.

And so we will.

Chapter 2
The Peloponnesian War

Thucydides was not the only person to write about the war. Divided after his death into eight long sections today called 'books', Thucydides' work breaks off in 411; his countryman Xenophon took up where Thucydides' unfinished manuscript left off. The comedies of Aristophanes provide a wealth of data about wartime Athens. The long *Library of History* composed many years later by the Sicilian historian Diodorus relied on the work of earlier writers that now is mostly lost, such as the 4th-century Athenian historian Ephorus and the slightly later Sicilian Timaeus of Tauromenium. Writing around 100 CE, Plutarch from Chaeronea in Boeotia north of Athens had access to a wide variety of sources now lost to us and wrote biographies of the Athenians Pericles, Nicias, and Alcibiades, and the Spartan Lysander. These works flesh out much that Thucydides omitted or chose not to discuss in detail. Plutarch's interest in personality and character led him to include anecdotes that bring participants in the war vividly before our eyes, and Aristophanes' opposition to the war provides an invaluable contrasting corrective to Thucydides' conspicuously pro-Periclean orientation.

The roots of the Peloponnesian War of 431–404 lay in the tensions that had arisen when the Greek world became a bipolar one following the foundation of the Delian League under the hegemony of Athens in 478. It was not the first time that the two camps had come to blows; there had also been a less bloody conflict that modern scholars call the First Peloponnesian War (460–445). As in many disagreements in Greece, the immediate trigger of this first war was a border conflict. The land bridge that linked the Peloponnesus with Attica and the rest of the mainland was occupied by the smallish polis of Megara. Around 460, quarrelling with its powerful Corinthian neighbour to the west, Megara defected from the Peloponnesian League and was received with delight into the Athenian alliance instead. Sparta and its allies did not take the defection of Megara well, and the fighting that broke out between the two leagues continued for 15 years.

Soon Athens had come to control all the territory of Boeotia to the north with the exception of the powerful polis of Thebes. For some years each side had mixed success in the war, but a defeat at Coronea in Boeotia in 447 brought an end to Athenian power there. Among the casualties at Coronea was Cleinias, a relative by marriage of Pericles. The two small sons Cleinias left behind soon found their home with Pericles. Both were reported to be little monsters, but the younger boy, Alcibiades, was handsome and disarming, and the Athenians were quite taken with him; even Socrates found him enormously appealing. His countrymen continued to find his antics engaging as he grew to adulthood, and he would go on to play a key role in framing Athenian policy. So great was Alcibiades' hold on the popular imagination that even after he defected to Sparta in 415 he continued to enjoy considerable support at Athens and was eventually welcomed back to the city—and elected to the board of generals.

Capitalizing on Athens's weakness after the defeat at Coronea, the Megarians slaughtered their Athenian garrison and returned to the Peloponnesian League. With the land bridge into Attica now wide open, the young Spartan king Pleistoanax set off for Athens at the head of an army. After a meeting with Pericles, however, he returned with his entire force to Sparta, where he was promptly exiled by his irate countrymen. Something remarkable had plainly transpired at that parley, and when Pericles' rivals and other enemies sought to discredit him, they found irregularities in his accounts that seemed to confirm the suspicion that he had bribed Pleistoanax.

Regarding peaces as essentially truces, the bellicose Greeks normally set expiration dates. The peace of 445 was to last 30 years and was thus known as the Thirty Years Peace, although in fact it endured for only half that. Its terms were five:

1. There was to be no further switching of sides.
2. Neutrals were free to join either side.
3. Each hegemon was free to make rules for the members of its own alliance and to use force to resolve conflicts within its own alliance.
4. Neither hegemon was to interfere in the league of the other.
5. Disputes were to be settled by arbitration.

The years that followed saw several abortive attempts to remove Pericles from his position of influence, including attacks on his common-law wife Aspasia, an immigrant from Miletus in Anatolia, and his friends the philosopher Anaxagoras and the sculptor Phidias. Pericles, however, withstood these attacks and was still the most influential member of the board of 10 generals when a domestic crisis in a remote outpost of Greek civilization erupted that would put the peace of 445 sorely to the test.

Tensions between democrats and oligarchs were not unusual in a Greek polis. Aristotle would observe in the 4th century that every city was in fact two cities, one of the rich and one of the poor. In 435 a civil war between the democrats and the oligarchs in the Corcyraean colony of Epidamnus in far north-western Greece prompted the democrats there to seek assistance from Corcyra (the modern Corfu). Rebuffed by their mother city, they turned instead to the state that had itself founded Corcyra 300 years before, 'grandmother' Corinth. Although most colonies had warm relations with their founders, Corcyra and Corinth had never got along, and it was probably out of sheer spite that the oligarchic Corinthians gladly agreed to champion the democrats' cause. Finding themselves at odds with Corinth, the Corcyraeans took advantage of the clause in the peace that permitted neutrals to join either side and sought an alliance with Athens.

Nervous as the Athenians were about offending Sparta's key naval ally, they were still more concerned that Corinth would defeat the Corcyraeans at sea and gobble up their substantial fleet, and the assembly took the risky step of accepting the Corcyraeans into their league. As was predictable, Athenians and Corinthians soon found themselves fighting one another, thus further imperilling the prospects for peace between the two leagues. Around the same time, the Athenians took action against the Megarians, but it is difficult to determine precisely what and why, for Thucydides gave the tensions with Megara conspicuously short shrift in his narrative. Evidently accusing the Megarians of harbouring escaped slaves and of cultivating some sacred borderland, the Athenians passed a decree excluding Megarian merchants from all ports of the Athenian Empire. As very few Greek ports of any significance stood outside the empire, Athens could thus cripple a member of the Peloponnesian League while still denying that it was in violation of the peace.

In the autumn of 432 the Corinthians denounced the Athenians before the Spartan assembly, portraying them as dangerously energetic and disturbingly ambitious. Though the Spartan king Archidamus urged his countrymen to build up their strength at sea before going to war with a powerful naval empire, the Spartans voted that the Athenians had violated the Thirty Years Peace, a decision followed soon afterwards by a vote for war on the part of delegates from the Peloponnesian League.

Yet no hostilities ensued. Despite their declaration of war, the Spartans sent to the revered oracle of the god Apollo at Delphi to enquire whether they should in fact take on the Athenians. Though they received encouragement, they nonetheless dispatched a series of embassies to Athens suggesting conditions under which the war could be avoided. The most serious among these was the rescinding of the decree against Megara, but they also made a point of demanding that the Athenians 'free the Greeks', that is, lay down their empire, an ultimatum clearly prompted by diplomatic motives: although there was not the slightest chance the Athenians would do this, the Spartans wished for it to be a matter of record that they were going to war to 'liberate the Greeks who are now enslaved', as their warmongering allies the Corinthians had put it. Though the Athenians were unmoved, the propaganda was by and large successful. It was largely for this reason, Thucydides maintained, that when the war broke out most Greeks were hoping for a Spartan victory. After several months of abortive negotiations, Sparta's impatient ally Thebes took the initiative in the form of a sneak attack on Athens's ally Plataea in the dead of night. From that point on, nobody could question that a state of war existed between the two alliances (Figure 2).

It would be a curiously asymmetrical war, for the Peloponnesian League probably had about a three to one advantage in infantry, the Delian League in ships. The Athenians were also far more experienced in naval warfare, and the Peloponnesian infantry surpassed that of the Athenians not only in numbers but in skill. Theban infantry—hoplites, as Greek infantrymen were called after the round shield they carried, the *hoplon*—were famous, and Spartan youths spent their lives in military camp training for war (Figure 3). In response to this imbalance, Pericles devised an ingenious strategy. Only the force of his personality and the eloquence in which it was grounded could have persuaded his countrymen to do something so dramatically at odds with human nature. Knowing that the Athenians' infantry was no match for that of the Peloponnesians, he convinced them to fight what was basically a war of attrition, albeit with the proviso that they would harass the Peloponnesians with their navy.

2. **Map of alliances during the Peloponnesian War.**

The Peloponnesian War

3. Line drawing of a Greek hoplite.

At Pericles' instigation, the farmers of Attica abandoned their rustic homes, taking with them only what could be loaded on a wagon, and joined the city dwellers inside the formidable Long Walls that linked Athens to its port Piraeus. Turning Athens into an island, as it were, the walls enabled food and other necessities to be brought to the populace by the imperial fleet that commanded the seas. Try as they might, the invading Peloponnesians would not be able to effect a battle with the Athenians, huddled safely within their walls. After a couple of fighting seasons that saw no combat, Pericles conjectured, the Peloponnesians would simply give up and sue for peace. The Spartans saw things differently. The Athenians, they imagined, would be unable to tolerate the frustration, not to mention ignominy, of allowing their land to be ravaged. They would either seek peace or flout Pericles' counsel and come out to fight—and lose. What nobody counted on was a horrific plague that attacked the city not long after the war broke out, carrying off about a third of the populace, including Pericles. Heartened, the Spartans were optimistic that the Athenians would give up, but they were mistaken. The war continued.

It was foreseeable that the preoccupation of the imperial navy with the war against the Peloponnesians would prompt rebellions in Athens's empire, and 428 saw the first of these when several cities on the island of Lesbos off the Anatolian coast rebelled under the leadership of the largest of them, Mytilene. When the rebels surrendered after a siege of nine months, the most influential of the politicians seems to have been the fiery Cleon, and at his instigation the Athenians voted to kill all the men and sell the women and children as slaves. The next day, however, many had second thoughts, and the debate that ensued in the assembly provided one of the most vivid scenes in Thucydides' *History*, with Cleon deriding his countrymen's indecisiveness and Diodotus, whose identity is uncertain, making a compelling argument for the ineffectiveness of the death penalty as a deterrent. It is chilling to read in the pages of Thucydides how the brutal first decree had just been read out in Mytilene when a second ship from Athens arrived, breathlessly announcing that the decision had been reversed—and that the death penalty would be imposed only on those who had actually participated in the rebellion. These were, Thucydides tells us, over a thousand men, but understandably this figure has been questioned; that would be a sizeable proportion of the adult male population. At around the same time, when the besieged Plataeans finally surrendered, the Spartans and Thebans killed the Plataean men and enslaved the women and children.

Civil wars, always endemic in Greece, became more common now that the democrats hoped to call in the Athenians, the oligarchs the Spartans. A bloody outbreak of civil strife in Corcyra in 427 was emblematic of the tensions that boiled over during the war years. Many oligarchic refugees from the violence, huddled in the temple of Hera, killed themselves there or hanged themselves from the trees outside rather than face a phoney trial at the hands of the democrats. So horrific was the bitterness between the partisans that fathers were even known to kill their sons.

The death of Pericles greatly increased the probability that the Athenians would abandon their fundamentally defensive strategy. The general Demosthenes persuaded his men to fortify the promontory of Pylos in the western Peloponnesus, which along with the narrow offshore island of Sphacteria enclosed the body of water known today as the Bay of Navarino (Figure 4).

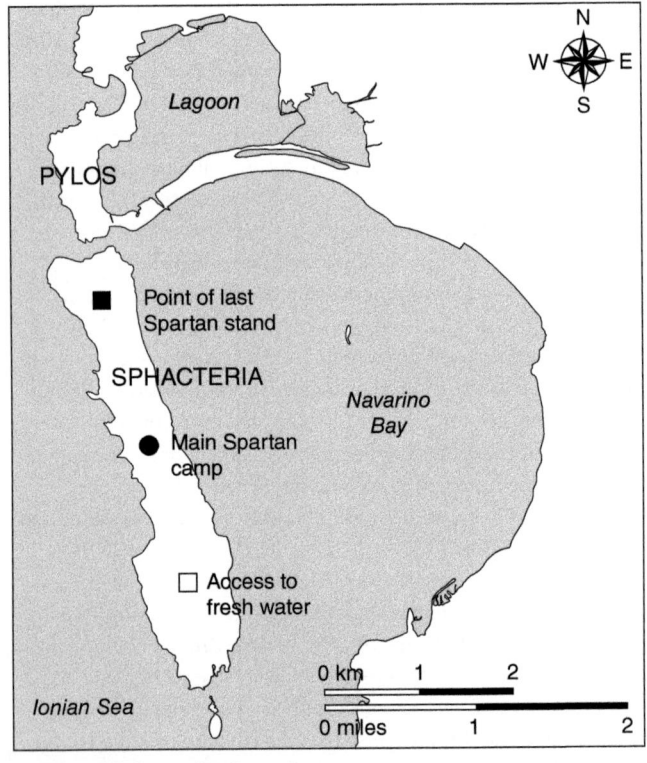

4. Map of Pylos and Sphacteria.

5. Shield of the Peloponnesians captured at Pylos.

Fearing that Sphacteria would fall into Athenian hands, the Spartans thought it would be a good idea to position a force of 420 soldiers on the island. It was in fact a dreadful idea. Led by Cleon and Demosthenes, the Athenian navy landed on the island, killing 128 of the Peloponnesian soldiers and capturing the remainder (Figure 5). Struggling with a declining population and horrified at the prospect of losing the survivors, the Spartans sued for peace, but, influenced by Cleon, the Athenians sent their envoys away.

The fortification of Pylos was not the only evidence that the Athenians were looking west. In 427 they sent an exploratory force to Sicily, and when the expedition amounted to nothing the three admirals in command were impeached. In the north, the eloquent and charismatic Spartan commander Brasidas brought a number of cities into the Peloponnesian League—resulting, as we have seen, in the impeachment of Thucydides. Whether he fled Athens to avoid the death penalty or was exiled we may never know. The deaths of both Brasidas and Cleon in 422 opened the way to the peace that was signed in 421 and named after its principal negotiator on the Athenian side, Nicias. Several key Spartan allies, however, refused to sign the peace, and although the hawk Cleon was dead, another Athenian with a major investment in the war had come of age: Pericles' rogue ward Alcibiades. At Alcibiades' instigation, Athens soon formed an alliance with Sparta's old rival in the Peloponnesus, Argos, and Sparta's disaffected allies Elis and Mantinea joined the alliance as well, but the Quadruple Alliance suffered a decisive defeat at the Battle of Mantinea in 418, the largest infantry battle of the war.

For reasons that are unclear, in 416 the Athenian navy sailed against the Aegean island of Melos, demanding that it join the empire. Thucydides reproduces a disquieting parley between the Athenians and the Melians in which the Athenians argue the futility of resistance and the Melians express the hope of deliverance, a sham negotiation that was really only the recital of harsh realities on the part of the Athenians. When the Melians refused, the Athenian assembly decreed death to all the men, enslavement for the women and children. This time there were no second thoughts (as there had not been when Scione in the north had gone over to Brasidas). It was in this atmosphere that Euripides produced his compelling *Trojan Women*, a play that, like *Lysistrata*, is still produced today in both its original format and in adaptations as a condemnation of war, as it underlined the horrors the women of Troy suffered at Greek hands after the city's fall.

Pericles had encouraged the Athenians to believe that they could win out against the Peloponnesians provided they became involved in no distractions, but by 415 Pericles was long dead, and when ambassadors from their old ally Egesta in Sicily came before the Athenians to seek support in a war with its neighbour Selinus, the temptation proved too great to resist. The Athenians also fell for a clever trick. When they sent an embassy to confirm that Egesta was in a position to help fund the expedition, the clever Egestans gathered together a set of precious gold and silver goblets not only from the town itself but from neighbouring settlements as well and passed it surreptitiously from one house to the other, so that when the men were entertained in private homes they came to the conclusion that the city must be fabulously wealthy (Figure 6).

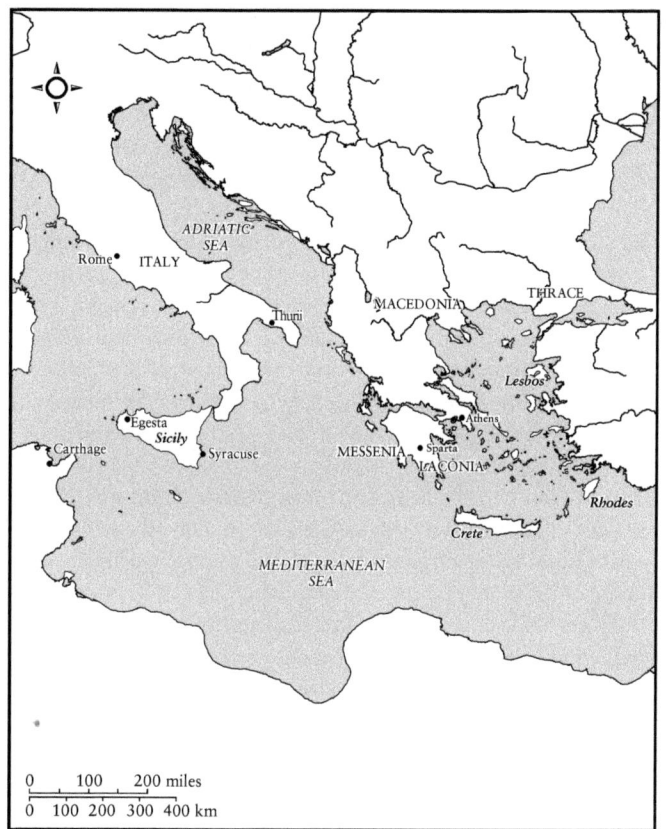

6. Map of Greek world including Sicily.

In vain did the cautious Nicias point out the imprudence of becoming involved in a struggle hundreds of miles away when Athens was still recovering from both war and plague and had enough enemies close by to worry about. Predictably, Alcibiades spoke in favour of the expedition, and his arguments won the day. Nicias' attempt to dissuade the Athenians by pointing out that they would need to send an enormous armada if they expected to accomplish anything backfired; they happily voted for the huge force. Off went tens of thousands of Athenians to Sicily under Alcibiades, Nicias (who the Athenians hoped would rein in Alcibiades' wild temperament—surely a strange idea), and a third general, Lamachus, dragging with them a huge number of subject allies and aiming ultimately to subdue the entire island.

The rakish Alcibiades, however, had got in trouble for revealing secrets about the cult of the goddess Demeter and her daughter Persephone, whose rites were celebrated by Greek-speakers from all over the world, and the Athenians were also in a panic after the nocturnal mutilation of the protective images of the god Hermes that stood throughout the city. A ship was dispatched to Sicily to bring Alcibiades home for trial, whereupon Alcibiades defected to Sparta, showing that he was not only a rogue but a traitor. When Lamachus died fighting, the expedition was left in the hands of Nicias, who was held back from effective action both by his cautious and vacillating nature and by a horribly painful disease in his kidneys. Misery abounded in the Greek world: Thucydides tells how the Athenians, hurting for money, decided to send home, unpaid, some Thracian mercenaries who had arrived too late to accompany the Athenians to Sicily. En route, they attacked the little Boeotian town of Mycalessus, killing men, women, children, even animals—every living thing they encountered. They even burst into a school where the boys had just entered and hacked them all to bits.

If the Athenians were to have success in Sicily, they would have to reckon with the most powerful state there, Syracuse. A jumble of Athenian walls and Syracusan counter-walls soon sprang up, and the two sides were at a stalemate when Nicias wrote home asking to be recalled because of his illness and indicating that only a force just as substantial as the original one would have any chance of success. Once again, he had failed to take the measure of his compatriots. They did not recall him, but they did send a huge second army under Demosthenes.

Not even the gifted Demosthenes was able to extricate the Athenians from a very tough spot. Alcibiades had instructed the Spartans to fortify a base in Attica and to send aid to the Syracusans in Sicily. They did both. When Demosthenes had finally persuaded Nicias that retreat was called for, there was a lunar eclipse, which many of the soldiers took as a bad omen, and the superstitious Nicias, who, Thucydides wrote, 'was overly inclined to believe in the interpretation of omens and the like', insisted on heeding the advice of the soothsayers, who declared that it was imprudent to move before 27 days had elapsed. The delay was fatal; the Syracusans went on to defeat the Athenians decisively in a naval battle in their harbour. Tens of thousands of Athenians and their hapless subject allies and slaves died for nothing.

The Athenians' miscalculations in Sicily sparked three major developments in the Greek world. The Spartans set about beefing up their navy; rebellions broke out across the empire; and an oligarchic coup at Athens overthrew the democracy in what had previously been an exceptionally stable state, though the democrats managed to oust the oligarchs and restore their government in less than a year. The theatre of war now migrated to the east, where the coast and offshore islands of Anatolia saw one naval battle after the other, with victories going sometimes to one side, sometimes to the other. Persian support became a possibility, and Alcibiades persuaded the Athenians to recall him through false promises that he could deliver it. For this phase of the fighting our principal source is Xenophon. Despite the devastating loss of ships and men, the Athenians held out for eight more years after the Sicilian catastrophe, during several of which the slightest shift in the balance could easily have resulted in their winning the war.

Both sides courted the support of Persia, the Spartans disgracefully betraying the Greek cities of Anatolia by agreeing to hand them over to the Persians. The Spartan high admiral Lysander formed a friendship with the young Persian prince Cyrus that ultimately proved fatal for Athens, as Persian gold enabled the Spartans to siphon sailors from the Athenian navy by the promise of better pay. The Athenians also deprived themselves once again of Alcibiades' services: when he left his fleet in the command of a personal friend who foolishly engaged Lysander's forces, losing 22 ships, he was deposed from office and fled into exile once again. At first, all seemed lost for Sparta when the Athenians scored a dramatic naval victory off the Arginusae Islands, but a powerful storm arose immediately after the battle, and worn down by decades of war, the Athenians in a frenzy voted to execute the eight generals who had neglected to pick up sailors living and dead from the choppy waters afterwards, thus narrowing the pool of experienced commanders. The trial, entailing as it did judging all the generals on a single slate, was illegal, and Socrates tried to stand in the way, but to no avail. Among the generals executed was Pericles the younger, son of the famous statesman.

Late in the summer of 406 Lysander made a surprise attack on the imperial fleet at Aegospotami in the Hellespont, capturing 171 of the 180 ships and cutting Athens off from its grain supply in the Black Sea region. Its ports besieged by the Spartans, a starving Athens surrendered a few months later. Lysander promptly installed an oligarchy of 30 pro-Spartan Athenians, who, according to the author of the *Athenian Constitution* (probably a student of Aristotle), 'refrained from harming none of the citizens, but put to death those who were outstanding with respect to wealth or birth or reputation, wishing to free themselves from that source of danger—and also wanting to plunder their estates; and by the end of a short interval of time they had done away with no less than 1,500'. These men came to be known to history as the Thirty Tyrants. One of the ringleaders was Critias, a pupil of Socrates. The oligarchs' excesses soon brought them down, prompting the Spartan king Pausanias to support the exiled Athenian democrats in their effort to retake their city. An amnesty was declared whereby only the Thirty and their immediate associates could be brought to trial for any crimes committed prior to 403, and the work of rebuilding post-war Athens began.

Chapter 3
Thucydides the historian

The 19th-century historian Leopold von Ranke famously proclaimed that the role of history was not to judge the past or instruct the present for the benefit of the future. Rather, it should simply aim to show how things really were. Thucydides saw things very differently. He most definitely sought to show how things really were, correcting the record where necessary, but he also sought to instruct the present for the benefit of the future.

Ironically, Thucydides' narrative, written at the very outset of the genre, was very much a revisionist history, composed with the purpose of offering a new paradigm that would replace the one current in his day placing all the blame for the war on Pericles and often ascribing his actions to discreditable personal motives. It was also a profoundly philosophical history, for Thucydides was a deeply thoughtful man. Why it was that history unfolds as it does is a question we all ask. A very curious people, the Greeks asked these questions too, and like people today, they came up with a variety of answers.

Composed perhaps in the 7th century but drawing on verses that had been handed down for many generations, Homer's *Iliad* had ascribed a large role to the gods, attributing the misery that resulted from a bitter quarrel between the Greek commander-in-chief at Troy, Agamemnon, and the best Greek fighter, Achilles, to the workings of a divine plan. Sing, goddess, he begins as he invokes the Muse,

> the wrath of Peleus' son Achilles
> That baneful wrath that brought such countless woes on the Greeks
> And sent so many stalwart souls of heroes down to Hades,
> But made their bodies a feast for dogs and birds,
> As the plan of Zeus came to fulfilment.

Though the gods are also intimately involved in the action of the *Odyssey*, the later poem presented a more modern view that places more emphasis on human action. Why was it that Odysseus arrived home alone after his many travels? His men all perished through their own presumptuous folly, punished for devouring the forbidden cattle of the sun god, Helios. Look, says Zeus to his Olympian family:

> How very quick those mortals are to blame the gods for everything!
> We are the ones, they say, who cause their suffering. Not true.
> It's they themselves who by their recklessness suffer far more
> Than necessary.

The 6th-century poet Theognis, on the other hand, ascribed tremendous power to the gods in determining a person's lot, writing,

> No one's the cause of his own loss or gain,
> But rather gods bestow them both; nor when
> We toil and labour do we really know
> Whether the outcome will be good or bad.
> . . .
> We mortals, knowing nothing, choose in vain:
> The gods drive all in keeping with their aims.

Herodotus was not prone to ascribing the course of history to divine meddling. His gods never materialize on the battlefield as they do in the *Iliad* or pop up at the dinner table as they do in the *Odyssey*. A strong sense of divine oversight, however, pervades his *Histories*. He tells the story of Pheretime of Cyrene in North Africa, who not only impaled men whom she suspected of complicity in her son's death but also decorated the city walls with the breasts she had chopped off their wives. Shortly afterwards, he wrote, 'she died horribly, teeming with maggots while still alive, as if to show people that excessive retribution will exact a proportionate response from the gods'.

The role of the gods in the lives of mortals was a frequent topic of Thucydides' contemporaries the Sophists. In defending the adulterous Helen, Gorgias adduced several possible reasons for her escapade. One was divine will: she could hardly be blamed if the gods had wished her to decamp with Paris to Troy. Another possibility, of course, is *erōs*—passion. If Eros is a god, with all the power divinity entails, how could a mere mortal refuse him? If, on the other hand, passion is a human sickness, it must be viewed as not a failing but a misfortune. Perhaps, though, she was persuaded by words. Even in that case, it is not difficult to defend her, for 'speech is a powerful master that with the smallest and least evident body manages to work the most divine feats ... How many men on how many subjects have persuaded and do now persuade many others by moulding a deceptive speech!'

Thucydides had strong opinions about why history unfolds as it does: it grows primarily from actions freely chosen by human beings themselves, individuals motivated sometimes by reason, sometimes by passion—and often by a deceptive speech. Undeniably, chance also plays a role. At no time does he suggest that either Athens or Sparta enjoyed the gods' favour or that setbacks might have resulted from courting divine anger. Nicias, when the Sicilian campaign has gone sour, seeks to hearten men with a pathetic speech in which he puts forward his own history of piety as grounds for hope and holds out the prospect that the army's sufferings may let up since 'even if it was one of the gods who begrudged us this expedition, we have paid a heavy enough penalty already'. After all, he muses, seeking desperately after palatable arguments, 'states that have attacked others in the past, as people will do, have been able to endure the punishment that attended on their conduct. So we now have reason to hope that the god will be kinder to us, as we are currently more deserving of pity than of envy.' Thucydides himself, however, never in his own voice hints at divine retribution as an explanation for the Sicilian disaster, and as we have seen, he took a dim view of Nicias' religiosity. One imagines Herodotus might have perceived the Sicilian debacle differently. Perhaps he did; the date of his death is uncertain, and he may have lived to learn of it.

The question as Thucydides saw it was not to what degree the course of events was divinely determined but rather what reasoning and what emotions moved people to act as they did. For him, as for other ancient historians, the course of history was shaped by people, not by impersonal forces (economic, institutional, social, environmental) as a modern historian might have it. Thucydides' Pericles was the embodiment of reason, his Archidamus prudence personified. His Brasidas is eloquent and intelligent but moved by personal ambition as well as patriotism; his death along with Cleon's opened the way to peace since both men had opposed any settlement—Cleon, Thucydides alleged (but he plainly hated the man), because his criminality would be laid open to view, Brasidas because he cherished the prominence the war was bringing him. In Thucydides' narrative, as in life, Alcibiades is something of a wild card, manipulative and self-interested but evidently an estimable general.

Did Thucydides subscribe to the Great Man theory of history and believe that the course of history was largely determined by prominent individuals? To some degree, yes. It is impossible not to see an element of that in the role he ascribes to Pericles of rescuing Athenian democracy from itself by his astute and unruffled leadership, but he was not unaware that Pericles' war strategy failed to take two important factors into consideration: the Athenians' restless temperament and his own mortality. Though Brasidas is also portrayed as a dynamic force, it was plain to Thucydides that his successes were problematic for the Spartans, who were troubled by the cult of personality that had arisen around him, and that it was only his death that made the peace of Nicias possible. And of course the opposite—the key role of the not so great man—was also evident in Thucydides' portrayal of Nicias' mind-boggling ineptitude with respect to Sicily, both in his inability to persuade the Athenians of the undertaking's foolishness and in his bungling of the campaign once it was under way.

Thucydides' focus on the war is a narrow one. Like sunshine concentrated in a convex lens, it causes his material to burn all the more brightly, but it also entails the loss of a wider picture. Political man is the only character in Thucydides' *History*, where women and slaves are conspicuous by their absence. We learn nothing from Thucydides about the hardships occasioned by the absence of men at war so pointedly depicted in Aristophanes' *Lysistrata* or indeed about the play itself. The text contains some three dozen appearances of the word 'slave', but nearly always in mentioning the hapless women and children of captured cities whom the victors rob of their freedom. Slaves in Thucydides are almost always victims, not actors, and the word is sometimes used figuratively, as when Cleon accuses the Athenians in the assembly of being 'slaves' to the arguments of clever speakers.

Thucydides' profoundly masculist text excludes both the family and what Greeks called the *oikos*, the household, consisting of husband, wife, children, and slaves. Aristotle in his *Politics* at times imagined the polis as consisting of households, but at other times of voters, that is, citizen males, and it is the latter construct that appears in Thucydides' *History*. Thucydides mentions hundreds of Greek men by name but fewer than ten Greek women; the omission of Pericles' high-profile common-law wife Aspasia is particularly striking. No slave is named in the entire course of Thucydides' narrative. It is worth noting that in both Thucydides' treatment of the plague and his discussion of the stasis at Corcyra family ties are ignored or perverted. In the first case people fear to visit their relatives, who often die in neglect, and those who suddenly inherit wealth scurry to spend it right away, not knowing how long they would live, rather than saving it as their children's patrimony. In the second, fathers kill their sons.

Thucydides' concept of history is limited to the actions of political man in his role as voter, office-holder, soldier, and commander in the field. The surgical precision of his focus results in the omission of much material of patent relevance to his topic. We would never guess from Thucydides' narrative that the orphaned Alcibiades was raised in the home of his relative Pericles, a connection that it would be quite useful to understand; that the embassy that prompted the Athenians' first, exploratory expedition to Sicily in the 420s was headed by the renowned Sophist and orator Gorgias himself, a fact that sheds light on the Athenians' increasing enthusiasm for fine speaking; or that the philosopher Socrates himself fought in two battles during the war and was not only the teacher of Alcibiades but his admiring friend.

It was integral to the Greek belief system that an impermeable boundary separated the psyche of the slave from that of the free man, and that fighting was the province of free men alone. Like Herodotus, who did his best to conceal the undeniable contribution of slaves at Marathon, Thucydides found the participation of slaves in warfare distasteful and glossed over it wherever possible. He reports that, following two victories over a Peloponnesian navy consisting primarily of Corinthian vessels, the Athenian admiral Phormio brought back to Athens such of the captives as were free men, making plain that some must not have been. Of slaves in the Athenian fleet, however, we read nothing. Thucydides, it seems, was averse to acknowledging the role of slaves in the armed forces of his own polis.

Though he does mention helots, his treatment of their wartime experience is revealing. When he recounts the Athenians' capture of the men on Sphacteria Island, Spartiate and helot alike, the helots mysteriously disappear from view. The Spartiate captives become high-profile POWs, valued pawns in international diplomacy, but Thucydides' narrative contains not a word about the fate of the helots whom the Athenians had seized. The one vivid detail he shares about the helots' experience in the Sphacteria campaign concerns the food brought to the Peloponnesian forces when they were stranded on Sphacteria in 425, when the Athenians agreed that the Spartiate soldiers would receive two quarts of barley meal, a pint of wine, and a piece of meat—but each helot only half that, even though the helots were no doubt equally ravenous. Thucydides' view of history had no room for the experience of the majority of people in Greece, those who were not male and free. Thucydides did great harm to history in more than one respect, reinforcing the notion inherited from Homer and Herodotus that a long narrative must have as its subject war—but, unlike them, concomitantly excising from history the experience of the vast majority of those caught up in it: women, children, slaves. 'In the absence of the householders, the farms were maintained by the redoubled labours of women and slaves,' said Thucydides never.

Within this narrow universe, Thucydides sees dynamic forces at work moving history forward. He begins his *History* by laying out the workings of these forces in the earliest days of Greek civilization in the section known as the Archaeology: the study of *ta archaia*, 'ancient things'. In its first centuries, he writes, the Greek world was plagued by instability as various groups migrated from one place to another, never putting down roots for fear of having their unwalled settlements raided by invaders. With people constantly fighting over the most fertile land, Attica with its thin topsoil was removed from the perpetual conflict. Soon identified as a stable and peaceful place, it became a magnet for migrants, who greatly increased the population.

The construction of a navy by the Cretan king Minos was a game-changer. Pacifying the Aegean by conquering the Cyclades and protecting his revenues by ridding the seas of piracy, Minos enabled people to amass capital by maritime trade. Thucydides' image of Minos as a maker of peace is at odds with the usual view of the Cretan king as a maker of war: the king's achievement evokes the Athenians' future status as a naval power, so that the two imperial naval powers can both be viewed as benefactors rather than conquerors. Enthusiasm for their newly acquired prosperity reconciled the weaker to the rule of the stronger, while the possession of capital made it possible for the more powerful to subjugate the weaker cities.

In his discussion of Minos, in other words, Thucydides presents us with an international order grounded in force but nonetheless advantageous even to the conquered. Subjection, he suggests, is an acceptable price to pay for the security and improvement in material circumstances that it entails. Force (or the threat of it) also explains for him Agamemnon's leadership of the expedition against Troy. Because of the strength of his navy, Thucydides maintained, fear was a major factor in the willingness of other Greeks to follow him. As the Greek world expanded after the Trojan War, their lack of unity prevented the Greeks from achieving anything substantial, the implication being once again that inter-polis organizations such as the Delian League fostered the well-being of the Greek world.

The themes that run through the Archaeology are the same ones that appear in Thucydides' explanation of the war's outbreak, fear and power. The truest explanation, he writes, 'although one wouldn't guess it from what the antagonists were saying, is that the increasing power of Athens and their fear of it drove the Spartans to war'. Much of that power, as in earliest times, lay in ships and money—and drive: *dynamis* is the Greek word, from which the English dynamic and dynamo are derived. In the Archaeology, in other words, Thucydides adumbrates several of the central themes of his *History* and sets forth his analysis of the dynamics of power, for which he sees three requirements: a financial surplus, a navy, and unification among various states under determined leaders.

It's immensely difficult to be certain when any given portion of the history was written. Thucydides said that he began writing as soon as the war broke out and continued year by year, but we know from asides that he fell behind and was often—but not always—writing with the benefit of hindsight. Clearly, though, he composed the Archaeology at a time when he anticipated that Athens, the wealthy naval power, would prove victorious in the war (Figure 7). But it did not. How did that happen? How did the sluggish tortoise Sparta outpace the agile Athenian hare? The answer to this question forms much of the *History*'s framework.

In Thucydides' construct, just as Minos' decision to build a navy was a dynamic force in the evolution of early Greece, the era we know as the Bronze Age, Athens is plainly meant to be perceived as

7. **Photo of a trireme under sail.**

the dynamic force of Thucydides' own era. The Corinthians at Sparta had sought to frighten their slow-moving hegemon into taking action by portraying the Athenians as high-energy go-getters beyond anything the sluggish Spartans could imagine, and in the funeral oration he delivered after the first year of fighting Pericles asked his fellow citizens to gaze upon the *dynamis*, the power, of Athens and fall in love with it (probably, I think, with the power, though possibly, depending on how one reads the Greek, with Athens itself). It is a powerful emotion Pericles is calling forth, and Thucydides accords a wide berth to emotion in its ability to drive human action.

Emotion appears in the funeral oration as a positive thing, depicted as the passion behind patriotism. In general, however, the historian bills it as a force that can upset the applecart of sensible policy and positive outcomes. He praises Pericles for manipulating the Athenians' emotions, writing that 'when the Athenians were in the grips of overconfidence he would frighten them back to good sense and when they had become irrationally frightened he would restore their confidence', but when discussing other speakers he is deeply concerned about the use of emotion to sway an audience. One of the dramatic contrasts Thucydides draws between Pericles and Cleon focuses on their differing interactions with the emotions of the populace. Pericles' goal is surely to whip the men in the audience up into such a frenzy of self-abnegating patriotism that they are willing to lay down their lives for their country, but we are plainly meant to think ill of Cleon when he concludes his speech on Mytilene by urging the members of the assembly to get as closely as possible in touch with the fury they felt when they first learned of the rebellion. Regarded by cooler heads as the enemy of prudence, white hot rage is here put forward as the best possible state of mind for decision-making. Diodotus in his response stressed the force of emotion over reason and the attendant dangers, as people carelessly give in to wishful thinking.

The historian would ascribe the same wishful thinking to the Athenian majority that supported the Sicilian venture of 415 against which Nicias had cautioned them so soberly, reminding them that they were just quit of one war and not yet fully recovered from the effects of the plague, and expressing concern about the 'mad passion for things beyond their reach' he feared in the young. Where Pericles had encouraged the Athenians to become lovers—*erastai*—of the city and her dynamic force, the Athenians disregarding Nicias' advice were instead swept off their feet by Alcibiades. 'Absolutely everyone was overcome by *erōs* [passion] for the undertaking.' Thucydides' narrative repeatedly bears out the Corinthians' caution to the Spartans that the Athenians 'are the only people in the world for whom achieving and hoping are virtually synonymous', for the flip side of optimism is wishful thinking and overconfidence. Athens is the wave of the future, but its energies become scattered and frenetic rather than focused; the portrait painted by the Corinthians, while designed to make the Athenians appear powerful, in fact pointed up their great weakness as well.

Among the most problematic emotions for Thucydides was pleasure, a feeling Thucydides engaged at the very outset of his *History* in his contention that the lack of entertainment value in his work might stand in the way of readers taking pleasure in it. The historian praises Pericles for not trying to acquire popularity by saying things that would give pleasure to the people; Nicias sends a letter home rather than relying on the speeches of his envoys, fearing that they might give an inaccurate report in hopes of pleasing the members of the assembly. Our actual achievements are so great, Pericles says, that we need no poet to give pleasure by inventing fictions. Under the strain of the plague, people indulged openly in pleasures they had once kept secret when they saw that one could be well one minute and at death's door the next; whatever felt good, that they deemed honourable.

Although Thucydides presents the unfolding of history as largely the product of decisions taken by mortal actors, he does not see these decisions as wholly responsible for the course of affairs. In addition to the dangerous effects of emotion, the wild card *tychē*, chance/fortune/luck, always lurks in the background, ready to strike at any time. Nobody who had lived through the plague at Athens could doubt the existence of an element of the incalculable. Greeks did not doubt that *tychē*, sometimes personified as a goddess, was a factor in the outcome of events. There is foresight, and then there is fortune, and in the interstices of that interplay history unfolds. Praised repeatedly for his foresight, a quality Thucydides valued highly, Pericles acknowledged that the plague was the one thing he could not have predicted, and the Athenian speaker at Sparta in 432 cautions his listeners about the element of the incalculable in war. A stunning naval victory in western Greece was due to a happy accident: when the admiral Phormio was commanding a squadron in flight from a pursuing Peloponnesian fleet, a merchant ship chanced to be lying at anchor ahead. Seeing his opportunity, Phormio immediately ordered his rowers to execute a sharp turn around the merchantman, a manoeuvre that made his ship temporarily invisible. When his trireme reappeared it was heading straight for the Spartan commander Timocrates' vessel, the flagship, which it immediately rammed. Sinking the ship, it threw the Peloponnesians into a panic and drove Timocrates to suicide.

Thucydides underlines the role of *tychē* in the fortification of Pylos in 425 that played such an important role in the war. When the Athenian fleet was off the west coast of the Peloponnesus, the other admirals were eager to get to Corcyra, where a Peloponnesian fleet had arrived, and they refused to let Demosthenes put in at the promontory of Pylos, but 'by chance a squall arose and carried the fleet into Pylos'. Chance soon intervened a second time. Demosthenes was unable to persuade either the generals or the men to fortify the spot as he had been hoping, but when no favourable winds arose and they found themselves becalmed, a burst of energy seized the restless sailors and the project got under way.

It is this mélange of reason and passion and dynamic force and chance that for Thucydides shaped the course of history. Frequently described as the world's first scientific historian, Thucydides has often been praised for the objectivity of his work. Both the characterization and the praise are misguided. Thucydides' work is neither scientific nor objective, for both notions rest on a misunderstanding of what the writing of history entails. History is not a science, and it cannot be objective, as it entails humans writing about other humans. Every omission, every connection, requires a judgement call. No historian can ever be proven to have demonstrated, in accordance with von Ranke's stated goal, how things really were, for that is something on which there can be no consensus. The day after Donald Trump's upset victory over the far more experienced Hillary Clinton in the American presidential election of 2016, I asked my ancient history students to come to the blackboard and each write a reason for Trump's success. The reasons varied widely—racism, misogyny, backlash against the previous administration, voter suppression—and none was mistaken; all the students had shown how, in their view, 'things really were', yet there was massive disagreement. Such is the writing of history, which, I am tempted to say, is more painting than photograph, but I will resist that temptation, since photography too is an art.

Chapter 4
Epic, tragedy, history

What precisely Aeschylus meant when he billed his plays as 'leftovers from the glorious banquets of Homer' is uncertain, but plainly the new genre of tragedy was a descendant of the vision that permeated the Homeric poems, a world of swirling strife in which some would win but others would lose; a world in which the very actions that brought heroes the renown for which they lived risked early death. If tragedy grew out of epic, the first two enduring historical works of Greece grew out of both. Organized around conflict and punctuated by the vaunting speeches of antagonists, heroic deeds, vivid battle scenes, and soldiers struggling to cope away from home and family, the works of Herodotus and Thucydides were profoundly coloured by the world of epic.

Herodotus' prose epic was built around the author's conviction that balance and order dictated that overreaching provokes an equal and opposite reaction in the form of retribution, sometimes human, sometimes divine—a schema, of course, that also figures prominently in tragedy. The notion that Xerxes brought his defeat upon himself by his hybris also figured prominently in Aeschylus' treatment of the war, *The Persians*. It would be surprising if a similar thought pattern did not shape Thucydides' work as well, and in fact despite Thucydides' marked lack of belief in the intrusion of the divine, his history was suffused with a profoundly tragic world view, one that pitted the congratulatory Periclean funeral oration against the ruinous plague that so eroded all civic and communal value, the savage massacre of the Melians against the catastrophic debacle in Sicily. Removing retribution as an obvious explanation does not change the fact that what goes up does have a nasty habit of coming down.

The *History* presents us with two competing narratives. On the one hand, the Archaeology shows a nexus of naval power, unity, money, and dynamic force moving Greece forward into modernity, a foreshadowing of Athenian modernity in Thucydides' own day. Thucydides lays out the Athenians' strengths in a way he never does those of the Spartans, first in three of the four speeches given at Sparta on the eve of the war, in which the Corinthians, the Athenians, and Archidamus each in their own way portray Athens as a formidable contender. Archidamus has much good to say about the Spartans too, but 'slow and steady wins the race' has a strong cast of wishful thinking about it, and subsequent events make clear that many Spartans were loath to take on Athens, as they seek reassurance from Delphi and send out repeated peace feelers.

Thucydides then shows us Pericles encouraging his countrymen by enumerating Athens's resources: the monies in the treasury, the ongoing imperial tribute, and an enormous quantity of precious metals in the Parthenon and other temples. By the time the Thebans strike the first blow at Plataea, readers have been primed to anticipate an ultimate Athenian victory. Only as the narrative progresses—and perhaps as the passing of time prompted Thucydides to amend his thinking—do we see that this forward motion ultimately leads to no good. The wealthy, forward-looking state grows drunk on its power and ultimately destroys itself. Now a different story unfolds, one that ends tragically in the harbour at Syracuse.

Yet the larger story is far from over. As Thucydides acknowledges early on, the Athenians make a striking recovery and come close to winning the war, holding out for years against a formidable array of opponents: their original enemies and the Sicilians who were now allied with them, their own rebellious allies, and ultimately the Persians, who had begun financing Peloponnesian operations. They did not surrender, he says, until they destroyed themselves by political infighting.

Thucydides' perception of the Athenian failure as multi-factorial undermines any easy pattern for tragedy just as it does any easy schema for political realism. At the same time, the presence of tragic elements is undeniable, and an overall sense that the Athenians have overreached at their peril pervades the *History*. The foreknowledge that Thucydides introduces by periodic narrative interventions echoes the experience of tragedy, in which the dismal outcome is known to the audience but not to the characters, and of course these interventions were reinforced by the lived experience of his readers. Greek readers would have been struck by the irony underlying Pericles' boast about the Athenians' law-abiding nature when, as Thucydides observed, a general lawlessness set in under the strain of the plague, when nobody expected to live long enough to be called to account for their actions; the decision to sail for Sicily sheds new light on the Athenians' dismissal of hope in their discussion with the Melians.

As in tragedy, action produces paradoxical results the very opposite of what was intended. In Sophocles' *Women of Trachis*, a jealous Deianeira sends her husband Heracles a cloak that she has been tricked into thinking will win back his affections. It is no such thing, and Heracles dies in agony. In Herodotus' mini-tragedy of Croesus, ruler of Lydia in Anatolia, the Delphic oracle had told the king that if he crossed the Halys River, he would destroy a mighty empire. Of course, it is his own empire that he destroys. Similarly Nicias' attempts to dissuade the Athenians from efforts against Sicily—first in 415 when he makes a speech outlining the enormous outlay of men and money that the campaign would require and again some time later when he sends a letter home describing the miserable condition of the expedition—backfire dismally. Tragic heroes often learn from experience, but Nicias does not.

The narrative is dotted with figures easily pegged as 'tragic warners', beginning with Archidamus, who advises the Spartans of the dangers of rushing into war without gathering more allies and, most of all, a navy; continuing with Pericles and his caution to the Athenians about not seeking to expand the empire during the course of the war; and then moving ahead to Nicias' reminders that the Athenians have only just recovered from the plague, that they have plenty of enemies close by about whom to worry, and that the force necessary for victory would be vast. Thucydides is a historian, not a dramatist, and he makes plain that the expedition was not in fact doomed from the start. When the Peloponnesian commander Gongylus arrived in 414, he reports, the Syracusans were on the brink of surrender. Nor does the Athenians' come-uppance play out neatly. Nicias, who had opposed the expedition, is executed, though he was, Thucydides wrote, the one Greek among all his contemporaries who, having demonstrated the greatest virtue throughout his entire life, least deserved such an unfortunate end. (I myself would not rate the bumbling general so highly.) Alcibiades, meanwhile, who lived to fight another day and then another and another, did not pay the penalty for his ill-considered grab at glory.

The heyday of Greek tragedy coincided with the lifetime of Thucydides. The tragedians had enshrined the practice evident already in myth of conveying lessons through stories, and this too was Thucydides' method. Plato found tragedy corrosive because of its grounding in powerful emotions, but Thucydides rarely describes the emotions of the characters in his *History*. Detailed descriptions of the protagonists' affective states congregate around two events, the plague and the Sicilian expedition. The plague, however, not being man-made, lies outside the boundaries of tragedy. The same cannot be said of

47

the Sicilian debacle. There Thucydides pulls out all the stops as he depicts the pathos of the calamity with a passion that rears its head only rarely in the *History*, although we have seen it before in the Corcyraean stasis, in the butchery at Mycalessus. The underlying dynamics are evocative of tragedy: seized by hybris, the Athenians whose commanders have just sneered at the Melians for trusting to hope do exactly that. The dismissal of the Melians' caution about what might happen if someone should get the upper hand over them will come back to haunt them as they trip over their own spears in the bloody, muddy Assinarus River while the Syracusans hurl down missiles from the riverbank above.

Reason and passion jostle one another in the *History* as they had done in Euripides' *Medea*, when the coldly calculating social climber Jason, in the process of abandoning his wife to marry the local princess, dismisses Medea's agitation as arising from characteristic female passion. Nicias speaks with the voice of reason, but the voluptuary Alcibiades fills the assembly with *erōs* for something new.

The echoes of tragedy are heightened and enriched by a parallel assimilation to epic. On the Spartan side, Brasidas is portrayed very much in the mould of a Homeric hero. As for the Athenians, Thucydides plainly sought to infuse the Sicilian expedition with epic undertones. The handsome, charming Alcibiades evokes Paris. Like the self-interested Trojan prince, the Athenian aristocrat drags his country and its allies into a ruinous war for personal reasons: an Athens at war afforded opportunities for his self-aggrandizement which an Athens at peace did not. Alcibiades avoids a death sentence at home by conveniently disappearing while en route from Sicily back to Athens, just as Paris avoids being killed by Helen's husband Menelaus by disappearing from the battlefield, whisked away in a mist by a protective Aphrodite. Both Paris and Alcibiades embody *erōs*—an *erōs* that Alcibiades manages to convey to the entire populace, with ruinous consequences. Thucydides also makes overt reference to Homer at the outset of his Sicilian narrative, mentioning that the legendary races of cannibalistic giants, the Cyclopes and the Laestrygonians, were reported to have been the earliest settlers of the island. His comment reminds us that Odysseus' wanderings were popularly believed to have included Sicily; many identified the narrow channel flanked by the monsters Scylla and Charybdis as the Strait of Messina that divides Sicily from Italy. The theme of return is prominent in both the Homeric poems: does it await the soldiers far away when the fighting is done, or will they be robbed of it by death or enslavement? It is a powerful word, *nostos* (return home), the origin of the English word *nost-algia*, literally pain in connection with the longing to return to a past life. The opening of the *Odyssey* defines Odysseus' motivation as staying alive and achieving the *nostos* of his comrades. All those comrades died—because, Homer says, of their own folly. After the defeat in the harbour the Athenians are terrified of being trapped in Sicily, and rightly so. In the very last paragraph of the Sicilian adventure, the dramatic conclusion of the narrative, Thucydides observes that of the many who had gone on the expedition, few ever returned to their homes. Folly takes many forms.

While sorrowful events alone do not constitute tragedy, tragedy is rife with sorrow, and the pathos of the Athenians' fate in Sicily is heightened by Thucydides' powers of description. Thucydides' vivid account of the expedition's last days makes a stark contrast with the non-description of the excruciating suffering of the Melians as the Athenian soldiers rounded up the populace, consigning the husbands and brothers, fathers and grandfathers, to execution and the women and children to enslavement in an unfamiliar land. Whether by accident or design, this was the very fate explored soon after the massacre on Melos in Euripides' *Trojan Women*. The fact that it took some time to compose a Greek tragedy makes it uncertain whether Euripides was responding to the events on Melos or simply the horrors of the war more generally; the Athenians had obliterated Scione in the same way some years before, though Thucydides mentions this horror only in passing.

Tragedy operated within a set of rules that precluded violence onstage, resulting in painful messenger speeches in which horrific scenes were described for the audience to imagine. An agitated messenger announces the death of the title character in Euripides' *Hippolytus*, a death made more excruciatingly painful for the audience as we and the chorus are aware that it was called down on him by his father Theseus under the misapprehension that Hippolytus had raped his wife. When Poseidon, in answer to Theseus' prayer, sends a savage bull against Hippolytus' horses, the messenger reports,

> Confusion reigned. The axle-pins all leapt
> Into the air; Hippolytus himself,
> Entangled in the reins, was dragged along,
> Bound in a knot that couldn't be untied.
> His head now smashed against the rocks, his flesh
> All torn, he uttered cries it hurt to hear.

Misinformation and insufficient effort to seek out the truth have led to Theseus' bad decision to sentence his son to death, much as misinformation and a parallel failure would lead the Athenians to death in Sicily. Most of the Athenians, Thucydides maintained, 'were ignorant about the island's size and the number of its inhabitants and had no idea that they were taking on a war only marginally less extensive than that with the Peloponnesians', and of course they had fallen for the Egestans' trick with the rotating goblets and concluded that they would enjoy substantial financial support in Sicily.

There has certainly been pathos before in Thucydides' narrative. We have felt it at Corcyra, at Mycalessus. But insofar as the *History* is the tragedy of Athens (and of Pericles, who, thinking he could control the Athenians and anticipating an early end to the war, gave no thought to a successor in the event of his death), the debacle in Sicily takes on added significance. As the messenger who reported the death of Sophocles' Oedipus observed,

> griefs freely chosen hurt the most by far.

Thucydides is at his narrative best in recounting the bitter denouement of the failed Sicilian campaign. Standing on the shore watching the fierce battle under way in the harbour, he says, the Athenian infantry were 'terrified about how things were going to turn out as they had never been before'. Everything hung on the success of their ships, and for a while the two sides seemed about evenly matched. Some men saw the battle from one angle, some from another, with the result that some shouted, 'We're winning!', while others cried out, 'We're losing!' The sailors reacted similarly until the balance swung decisively to the Syracusans. At that point the infantry broke out in a shriek of unprecedented horror. These men, Thucydides wrote, now experienced something parallel to what the Spartans had at Pylos and Sphacteria Island, where, with the Peloponnesian fleet wiped out, the men on the island were finished. Now the Athenians had no hope of saving themselves barring a miracle.

The lack of hope of course brings us back to Melos in 416 and to the Athenian assembly in 415. Now the Athenians who had derided the Melians for their optimism are horrified to find themselves in straits that admit of no hope. Instead of subduing their new adversary, they are in exactly the same spot into which they had forced their old one. The Athenians who had disdained religion on Melos now find themselves led by a man who relies on it, and as the army makes a break for it, hoping to escape over land, the wounded cry out for succour not only to their departing comrades but indeed to the gods. Neither plea was answered. The Athenians who survived the next few days were consigned along with their allies to the dank quarries of Syracuse, where, subsisting

on a cup of water and two cups of ground meal a day, they endured
the stench emanating both from the makeshift latrines and from
the steadily growing pile of their comrades' rotting corpses.
Many of those corpses belonged to men who had been forced to
take part in the expedition against their will, but conspicuously
absent amid the pathos is any expression of particular compassion
for the hapless allies and slaves the Athenians had dragged to
their deaths in Sicily, men who, unlike the voters in the assembly,
had no say in their fates.

Thucydides does not leave it to his readers to draw their own
conclusions about the turnaround in the Athenians' fortunes,
one worthy of any tragedy. This, he says,

> was the greatest reversal that had ever befallen a Greek army, as
> the people who had come to enslave others were now fleeing for fear
> of suffering the same fate themselves. The expedition to Sicily was
> the largest campaign in the war—indeed, as far as we know, ever
> in Greek history. It was also the most glorious for the victors and the
> most disastrous for the vanquished. For the Athenians were totally
> defeated in every way. Ships, men—absolutely everything was lost.

Reversal of fortune, of course, was key to tragedy, and a central
element in Herodotus' tragedies of Croesus and Xerxes. Ideally
positioned to win the war, Athens instead loses both the war and its
empire. What could better represent reversal of fortune for
Thucydides' contemporaries than the fall of Athens?

Chapter 5
Thucydides the narrator

If Thucydides was really concerned that readers would find his war monograph dull, lacking as it did the charm of a Homer or a Herodotus, he need not have worried. War is rarely charming, but it is not for that reason uninteresting, and it is certainly not unexciting. Replete with plots and counter-plots, desperate marches, missed opportunities, and last minute reprieves, Thucydides' account of the war is anything but dull. Grounded as it is in his fascination with human nature, it cannot but hold the attention of his readers, who are, after all, human beings themselves.

The palette in which Thucydides depicts the war is very dark indeed. War, as he wrote, 'is a violent teacher'. Recoiling from what he perceived as the vagus nerve of civilization collapsing in on itself, he sought to capture in prose how and why this frenzy of killing took root in his lifetime and dragged not only his native Athens but countless other Greek cities down to new depths of savagery. It is an interesting pastime to speculate what Thucydides would have done with his energies had the war not broken out. International affairs plainly compelled him as a laboratory in which to explore human nature, and he might well have sought a career in politics and diplomacy. Perhaps he would have found his *métier* exploring the human condition on the tragic stage—or beaten Plato to the punch in composing philosophical dialogues. But the war did break out, and the rest is, literally, history. Overcome with horror at the events he saw unfolding, he gives us a *Guernica* of the 27-year conflict that amounted to the Greek world war.

Unlike the poets, Thucydides cannot claim the muses as a source of his information and understanding, and he is careful to establish his credentials as a narrator, stressing the fact that he was an adult at the time the war broke out, lived through it—and is very bright. He is not shy about setting himself apart from—and above—the run of human beings as he expresses his exasperation at the ease with which ordinary people accept falsehoods unquestioningly, listing a number of silly things that the average person believes, such as that each Spartan king had two votes in the Council, while in fact each king had one. This sort of thing he complains, 'proves how little effort most people put into their search for the truth, preferring to latch onto easy, ready-made answers'. He also signals his keen intellect by announcing that he recognized that the war was going to be something remarkable as soon as it had broken out. He has given serious thought, he makes clear, to the question of methodology, both in the reconstruction of speeches he had not heard and in the reconstruction of facts. Most of all, he establishes his authority by the manner in which he presents his material.

Expressions like I imagine, I believe, I suspect are largely lacking in Thucydides' text. In the course of the war, things simply happen, a phenomenon that leaves the reader with the distinct impression that there is no uncertainty in the *History* regarding matters of fact, no daylight separating the mind of the narrator from the events he reports; Thucydides appears to be not so much reconstructing and interpreting as simply transcribing. His approach makes a marked contrast with Herodotus, in whose *Histories* the word *legetai*, 'it is said...', appears over a hundred times. Thucydides is interested in what is, not in what is said. He frequently identifies the war as the one he wrote up: thus the war becomes synonymous with his account of it.

Throughout the bulk of the *History* Thucydides seeks to efface himself from the narrative, creating the illusion that the story is simply telling itself. In this he echoes Homer, who never said,

And then swift-footed Achilles challenged the king Agamemnon,
As most people have it; but others say the challenger was Odysseus...

Of course not. First person utterances, accordingly, are rare except when Thucydides is discussing his methodology at the outset of the work, speculating about the distant past, or making conjectures about the future. We are a little startled when the historian intrudes himself into the narrative, as when he talks about having had the plague himself and having observed others who were suffering from it. For this reason we pay close attention to the occasional first person intrusions when he speaks out strongly in his own voice, as when he lays out his explanation of the war:

I believe, however, that the truest explanation of the war—though one wouldn't guess it from what the antagonists were saying—is that the increasing power of Athens and their fear of it drove the Spartans to war.

The first person interventions are striking by their very rarity, as when he writes on the occasion of the death of Ambraciot soldiers in 426 that 'I have not even put down the number of the dead, because the number believed to have been lost beggars belief in proportion to the size of the city.' This observation, of course, does double duty, highlighting not only the degree of the disaster but Thucydides' own scrupulousness as a historian.

Thucydides' prose can be remarkably vivid. His picture of the fortification of Pylos brings the scene alive before our eyes, as the bored and becalmed sailors finally decide that they might as well fortify the promontory as sit idle. Having no suitable tools, they apply themselves to the project: 'picking up stones and putting them together wherever they happened to fit, and when they needed mortar, they carried it on their backs from want of pots, bending over that it would stay on and clasping their hands together so that it would not fall'. Brilliantly he made the decision to describe the decisive battle in the harbour of Syracuse not only from the point of view of the sailors but also from that of the anxious Athenian infantry looking on from the shore: those whose eyes were fixed on a spot where things were going well took courage while those who were focused where it was going badly cried out in terror until the Syracusans at last proved victorious, sparking a panic in the Athenians greater than any they had ever known. His skill in enabling readers to visualize a situation reached its peak in the final collapse of the retreating Athenians at the Assinarus River. The passage is well worth quoting at length (see Box).

Thucydides

When day broke, Nicias led his men forward again, the Syracusans and their allies pressing hard upon them in the same way, pelting them with spears from every side. The Athenians pushed on to the Assinarus River, not only because they were being harried by the spears, arrows, and stones coming from every direction and by the hordes of cavalry and other troops and thought that they would be in a better situation if they could just get across the river, but because they were exhausted and thirsty. When they reached the river, they broke ranks and charged into it, each man struggling to be the first to get across even as the enemy was making it as difficult as possible; but compelled to cross in a mass, they fell upon one another and trampled each other underfoot. Falling among the spears and equipment some died at once, while others getting entangled with their gear and with one another were carried away by the river.... The Peloponnesians came down into the riverbed as well and killed them, mostly right there, with their swords. And the water was quickly fouled; but the Athenians nonetheless fought with one another for the water contaminated with blood and muck.

Finally, when many bodies lay piled one upon another in the riverbed and part of the army was destroyed there while the few who had escaped were cut off by the cavalry, Nicias surrendered himself to Gylippus, whom he trusted more than he did the Syracusans, and told Gylippus and the Spartans to do with him whatever they wanted, but to stop killing his men.

This passage is about as close as Thucydides gets to depicting the process of dying, which after all is what makes war different from politics. In portraying the moment of death he is even more sanitary than Herodotus, who rather enthusiastically reports lurid executions and mutilations, usually perpetrated by non-Greeks whom Greeks perceived as going in for that sort of thing, but is quite perfunctory in his treatment of deaths in combat. The contrast with Homer is striking. As the war rages before Troy, heads roll in the dust, eyeballs pop out, tongues are speared, and the grief that will soon overcome bereaved parents is frequently noted. For the 5th-century historians, however, soldiers who lose their lives in battle are fundamentally just cogs in the wheel of statistics. The *History* afforded many opportunities for chilling accounts of death, opportunities Thucydides chose to forgo. What was going on in Mytilene when the second trireme arrived, bringing news of the reprieve? The general Paches had just read out the original resolution decreeing death to all males, enslavement to all women and children. Surely the second ship came upon a scene of mass terror, but of this we hear nothing. Thucydides seems very well informed about the phony negotiations on Melos; did his informants not also tell him exactly how the mass executions proceeded? The Athenians, he reports, executed all the grown men they could get their hands on. Plainly, then, there were some successful escapes, born of the deepest desperation. How did they kill them? Each one upon his capture, or were they led away in a bunch and executed as at Plataea?

Did the wives and mothers and sisters and sons and daughters observe the killing? What did they say, what did they do? Surely at the least they were witnesses to the capturing. But this is not the movie version. It is the Thucydidean version, and we are left completely in the dark.

Along the same lines, characters in Thucydides' *History* are not fully fleshed out. Rather they represent certain principles, certain types rather than individuals with well-developed personalities; they draw our interest not for what sets them apart from others but rather for the characteristic patterns of thought and action that they represent. Similarly with characters in tragedy: we never learn whether Jason had a bad back or if Oedipus was partial to anchovies: idiosyncrasies only serve to obscure the universality of the challenges at hand. Thus Archidamus represents the best in Sparta, Sthenelaidas the worst. Whereas Pericles embodies the union of wisdom and charisma, Nicias personifies prudence vitiated by an excess of caution; Alcibiades in turn encapsulates daring compromised by narcissism. It is easy to feel that Nicias was born old, Alcibiades a perpetual adolescent. Cleon, who was plainly active in Greek politics during Pericles' lifetime, is introduced only in the context of the debate over Mytilene. As he embodies rashness and crudeness and braggadocio, so it is in the context of a provocative and extremist speech that we first meet him.

The anecdotes in Plutarch's lives of Pericles and Alcibiades give us a far greater sense of what it would have been like to converse with these men over dinner than anything in Thucydides' work, as Plutarch gravitated to memorable vignettes revealing of not only character but personality. It is in Plutarch that we read that Pericles in his desire for power in the state broke off a variety of social relationships to avoid overexposure; that Alcibiades cut off his dog's tail so that the Athenians in focusing on the poor dog would lose track of his other faults. Despite Thucydides' patent contempt for Cleon, we must turn to the *Constitution of the Athenians* by Aristotle or one of his students to learn that Cleon 'was the first person to shout and revile those who disagreed with him on the platform, and to pull his cloak around him before making a speech, unlike everyone else, who spoke in a decorous manner'. Cleon has no backstory. We learn nothing about who his allies were, or how he rose to prominence despite a background many found suspicious. Other sources indicate that he had a contentious relationship with Pericles, but we learn nothing about this from Thucydides.

A participant in this war as well as its historian, Thucydides would have been made of stern stuff indeed if he had been able to produce a completely impartial account of his own involvement in the fighting. In the event, he did not. The Spartan general whose skilful campaigning ended Thucydides' career in the military is at every turn built up into a formidable opponent: determined, dynamic, charismatic, tireless, and eloquent. Thucydides begins to develop Brasidas' character upon his first entry into the narrative, only shortly before the disaster at Amphipolis; we can infer that Amphipolis had already been lost when Thucydides reached this point in his narrative, and that he knew as he detailed the heroism of Brasidas at Pylos in 425 that he was describing the man who would change his life.

Brasidas was, Thucydides says, the most conspicuous among the Spartans. Seeing the other captains hanging back, intimidated by the rugged terrain and worried about wrecking their ships, he shouted that it made no sense to fret over a pile of timber when the enemy had erected walls on their soil. Force a landing, he cried, even if it means ruining the ships! And after he had made his own pilot run their ship aground and was trying to climb down onto the land, he was wounded so badly that he fainted and tumbled into the outrigger, his shield slipping into the sea to be retrieved by the Athenians for use in the victory trophy they would later erect. The word Thucydides uses for Brasidas' swooning is *elipopsuchēse*; it appears nowhere else in his narrative but often in Homer, and in fact, unlike other commanders who figure in the *History*, Brasidas is cast in a heroic, indeed Homeric, mould.

Alcibiades in Plato's *Symposium* would compare Brasidas directly to Achilles. Like Achilles, whose tutor Phoenix had been charged with teaching him to be a speaker of words and doer of deeds, Brasidas (like Pericles) receives praise from Thucydides for both his eloquence and his acts: not a bad speaker for a Spartan, Thucydides says in a dramatic understatement, and *drastērios*: energetic, a doer. Upon his death he became the object of a cult at Amphipolis, something Thucydides reports of no other war hero. He was buried at the public expense, and the people of Amphipolis built an enclosure around his grave, made annual sacrifices to him as to a hero, and established lavish athletic competitions in his honour.

Thucydides relates the progress of Brasidas' speedy march through Thrace and tells how he brought Athens's ally Acanthus over to Sparta with a mixture of mellifluous words and ominous threats. Nearby Stagirus (the future birthplace of Aristotle) soon joined in the rebellion, as did Argilus (Figure 8). By the time Brasidas is braving the snow to cross the bridge over the Strymon River that leads to the city, we are well acquainted with his unbroken record of successes: he is a veritable tsunami sweeping through the north. Thucydides' words throughout are very carefully chosen. When Brasidas arrives at the gates of Amphipolis, Thucydides reports, having overpowered the guards on the bridge, the citizenry was divided as to whether to let him in, and in concert with Eucles, the Athenian general in charge, those who did not wish to surrender 'sent to the other commander in Thrace, Thucydides, son of Olorus, the author of this narrative, who was at the island of Thasos, a colony of Paros, half a day's sail away, instructing him to come to their aid'.

He offers no explanation for his absence on an island which required no protection from Brasidas, who had no ships.

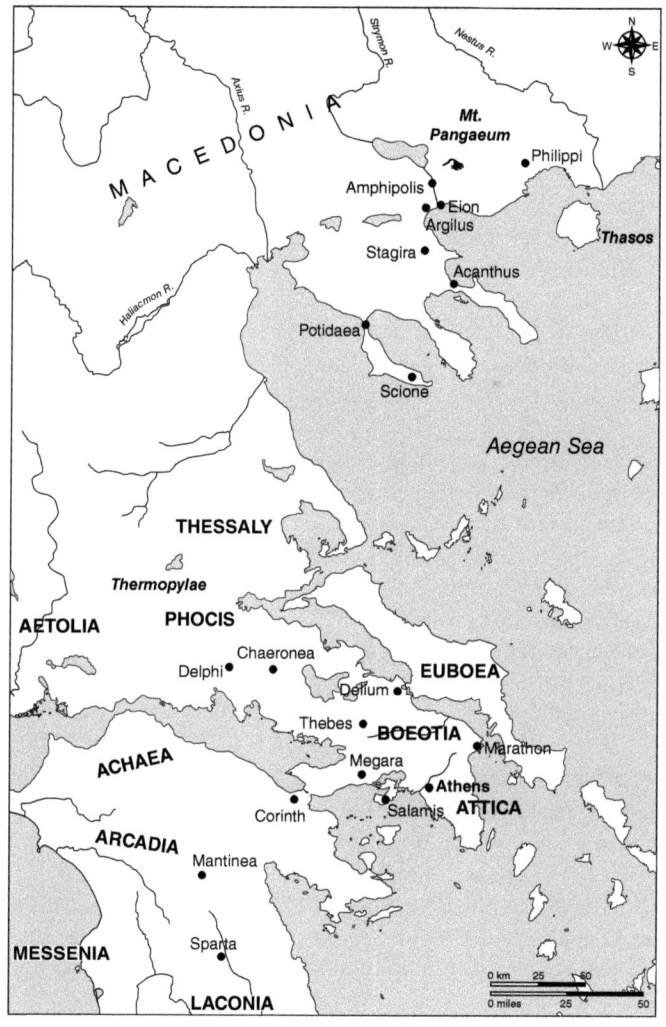

Thucydides the narrator

8. Map of the Chalcidic peninsula.

Thucydides set sail at once, we read, hoping to reach Amphipolis in time to save it, or at least to preserve Eion. Brasidas, meanwhile, worried about the impending arrival of Thucydides and concerned that Thucydides' inherited mineral rights in the area probably gave him great influence with prominent citizens on the mainland, offered the Amphipolitans very modest terms if they would surrender—as in fact they did, especially since the residents of Amphipolis, an Athenian colony, came from all over, only a small number being from Athens. Later that very same day Thucydides sailed into Eion and secured it such that the attack of Brasidas was futile. Had Thucydides not arrived so quickly, he stresses, Brasidas would surely have possessed Eion as well, but as it was he had to settle for Amphipolis.

The possession of Amphipolis could hardly be labelled settling. The jewel in Athens's northern crown, Amphipolis was strategically located, commanding a path through Mount Pangaeum and a bridge over the Strymon River and offering access to timber as well as gold and silver mines. The Athenians were so devastated by its loss that they either exiled Thucydides or sentenced him to death *in absentia*. Recovering Amphipolis was a crucial part of their dealings with the Spartans for many years, and for all their efforts, it never did return to Athenian hands.

What Thucydides was doing off at Thasos remains a mystery, but had the explanation been creditable he would surely have shared it with us. The Athenians were incensed with good reason. Much as it pains me to say so, it seems probable that Thucydides was attending to the gold mines to which he held the rights or to some other private interest. As for Brasidas, the capture of Eion would for him have been merely the icing on the cake and represented no great loss. To hear Thucydides tell it, however, Amphipolis was a soft target because of its mixed population; even so, Brasidas offered exceptionally lenient terms because he was so afraid of the very influential Thucydides (the only instance of Brasidean fear in Thucydides' text).

Thucydides then rescued Eion by the alacrity of his response. Brasidas, he wishes us to understand, was not the only general at work in the north who moved quickly!

By casting Brasidas as an extraordinary individual, indeed larger than life, and by an account of the Amphipolis affair calculated to distract from his own failing—his exile is not even mentioned for many paragraphs, and then by way of an aside—Thucydides presents a narrative that makes the loss appear practically inevitable. Brasidas' adventures in the north entailed one success after another, and in rescuing Eion Thucydides managed to turn back a commander who was practically a force of nature. No wonder Thucydides could not outsmart Brasidas, who was not only a great general but indeed a Homeric hero.

The same calculation is evident in Thucydides' treatment of Pericles. The softening filter through which Thucydides presents Pericles and his position in Athens makes understanding what was really happening in the city into quite an arduous struggle. Other surviving sources (principally the comic dramatists) suggest that the Athenians held Pericles responsible for initiating the war and blamed him for the failure of his strategy as well. Greek drama both tragic and comic was integral to Athenian civic life. The state sponsored the festivals at which plays were performed before audiences of thousands, dramas that explored central issues facing the democracy: the relationship of the individual to the community, tensions between the sexes, the conflict between religion and the state, the implications of war, the nature of power. Because much of the dialogue on the comic stage was reminiscent of what one hears today on late night television, offering topical humour alluding to current hot button issues and merciless criticism of public officials, comedy provides a valuable corrective to Thucydides' rosy view of Pericles and his policies. In Aristophanes' *Acharnians* the farmer Dikaiopolis ('just city') seeks to make a private peace with the Spartans, as he has no quarrel with them. In Dikaiopolis' comic version of the war's causes, some drunken Athenian youths carried off a prostitute from Megara, whereupon the Megarians in turn carried off two prostitutes from a brothel run by Aspasia, prompting Pericles to introduce the decree against Megara. The Athenians refusing repeatedly to repeal the embargo at the request of the Spartans, war ensued.

Clearly the joke plays on the abduction of Helen by Paris, and it probably also parodies the opening lines of Herodotus' *Histories*, which report Persian tales of reciprocal woman-snatchings, culminating in the abduction of Helen, as precursors to the Trojan War. It points, however, to a genuine belief among many Athenians that the Megarian decree was the principal cause of the war and Pericles the principal cause of the decree. There was much truth to this, but Thucydides, disbelieving it and wishing to distract from Pericles' responsibility for the ruinous war, skims over it lightly. The first we hear of the tension with Megara is when the Corinthians, trying to dissuade the Athenians from allying with Corcyra, argue that war is not inevitable and suggest that 'it would be a good idea for you gradually to remove some of the suspicions to which your actions concerning Megara have given rise'. We next discover that the Peloponnesian allies who came to address the Spartan assembly included the Megarians, who had a number of complaints, 'in particular the fact that they were being excluded—in violation of the treaty—from harbours in the Athenian empire and from the Athenian agora'. Only later do we learn of the Athenians' grievances: 'that the Megarians were cultivating sacred ground, not respecting the border between the two states, and sheltering runaway slaves'. These scattered references have resulted in much spilt ink on the part of scholars trying to reconstruct what exactly happened: Geoffrey de Ste Croix's chapter on the Megarian decrees in his book on the origins of the war is some two-thirds as long as the book you are reading now.

Admiring Pericles as he did, and believing as he also did that the underlying cause for the war was the Spartans' fear of the

Athenians' growing power and not a spat over Megara, Thucydides deployed a variety of strategies for minimizing Pericles' central role in bringing on the unpopular war—and the opposition his policies faced on the home front. When the question of averting the war by rescinding the Megarian decree has come before the assembly, Thucydides includes a rousing speech by Pericles against rescinding the degree but not the speeches that he himself acknowledges were given on the other side. We do not even learn the names of the men who spoke or the gist of the arguments they put forward. In 430 Pericles was deposed and fined. The machinery for impeachment would of necessity entail several speeches: for and against the deposition, for and against Pericles at the trial that ensued. Probably there were a good number more. Yet we hear nothing of either the speakers or the speeches at this critical juncture in Athenian history. As to Pericles' strategy for winning the war, Thucydides, who elsewhere shows enormous sensitivity to matters of money, neglects to mention that the Athenians' resources, which Pericles himself has enumerated, were adequate to fund a war of two or three years but not one year more, a fact that did not cast Pericles' determination to go to war in the best light. He does, however, include an impassioned speech on Pericles' part complaining of the Athenians' lack of faith in him, contrasting the Athenians' vacillation about the war with his own constancy—'I am the same man; I have not changed my position'—and cautioning them that in their empire they are holding a tiger by the tail: 'You possess your empire like a tyranny, and while taking it may have been wrong, it would be extremely dangerous to let it go.'

Thucydides' conviction that the real cause of the war was the fear inspired in the Spartans by the growth of Athenian power leads him to trace the rise of Athens after the Persian wars as setting Greece on an inexorable path to war. For this reason, he reports none of the speeches made in the Athenian assembly arguing against the alliance with Corcyra, none of those that advocated rescinding the Megarian decree. As his own narrative makes clear, however, a very different story could have been told. That the

Thirty Years Peace was in fact quite promising is indexed by the caution the Athenians demonstrated in billing the settlement at Thurii in south Italy in which they were involved in 443 as a panhellenic colony. In 440, when Samos had rebelled from the Athenian Empire, the Corinthians, the most likely party to be provoked by the settlement at Thurii, argued before the Peloponnesian League that they should not take the opportunity to attack Athens. As Thucydides' narrative makes clear, moreover, significant factions in both Athens and Sparta favoured peace, including two Spartan kings, Pleistoanax and Archidamus. So hesitant were the Spartans to move forward with the war that they sent to the oracle of Apollo at Delphi asking whether they should go to war even after they and their allies had voted for it. By omitting the speeches delivered in Athens in favour of preserving peace by rescinding the Megarian decree, Thucydides makes it seem as if the path to war was the only one. In fact, had the Athenians taken the Spartans up on their offer to call off the war should the decree be retracted, the ensuing rage of the Corinthians at their hegemon would surely have worked to Athens's advantage. The course of the 5th and 4th centuries might have been radically different.

Modern scholars have labelled Thucydides' history 'intensely personal' and, alternatively, 'severely impersonal'. Thucydides would probably have preferred the latter characterization, but I lean towards the former. Not only is his narrative a *cri de coeur* on the part of a man who saw his universe collapsing around him; the account of the war that sprang from his pen—or stylus—is very much organized around his own very distinctive views of the events, and, unlike Herodotus, he feels no compulsion to lay out alternative hypotheses from among which we may take our choice. The illusion of objectivity that marks his text is just that. He has brilliantly arranged his material in such a way as to leave readers with the impression that he is simply telling us 'what happened', but there are other ways of interpreting these events, and through countless calculated choices he distracts our attention from such alternatives.

Chapter 6
Speeches in Thucydides

Thucydides laid out his methodology at the outset of his work. Where determining the facts was concerned, he had taken care not to be satisfied with the first source that came to hand. Rather, he had made a careful synthesis of what he himself had witnessed and what he had heard from others, always assessing the accuracy of reports with the greatest effort and care. With respect to speeches, on the other hand, some of which he had heard himself and some about which he had learned from others, it was always difficult to remember them word for word, and consequently he has included in his history what it seemed to him that the speakers must have said given the situation in which they found themselves—sticking of course as closely as possible to the gist of what was actually said.

This discussion of the challenges involved in reconstructing speeches is unique among ancient historians and makes a striking contrast with the breezy assurance with which others both before and after Thucydides inserted into their narratives speeches that they had plainly never heard, as when Herodotus blithely reports verbatim what the Persian queen Atossa said to her husband Darius in bed to encourage him to attack Greece. In the prominent place they gave to speeches in their work, Thucydides and Herodotus followed the lead of Homer, particularly in the foundational war narrative of Greek civilization, the *Iliad*. Some speeches that appear in the *History* Thucydides plainly heard himself. Most he did not, and inevitably we are plagued by curiosity as to the identity of his informant—a curiosity that is never likely to be satisfied, though it is hard not to suspect that the historian spoke with Brasidas, about whose motives and thinking he appears to know so much, and perhaps Alcibiades and Demosthenes as well.

The *History* contains over 40 speeches, and dozens more are reported indirectly. Through them Thucydides sets out the issues that exercised the minds of the participants in this war, and many that must exercise those of participants in any war. They are so central to his work that the very minor role they play in Book 8 has suggested that it may have been unfinished. Though many speeches stand alone—Thucydides never depicts anyone responding to Pericles—pairs and other groupings are common. Of six sets of paired verbatim speeches, three were delivered back to back to the same audience. The Corcyraeans and Corinthians plead their cases before the Athenian assembly in Book 1; Book 3 contains two parallel debates on matters of life and death, one between Cleon and Diodotus on the fate of the Mytileneans and one between the Plataeans and the Thebans concerning the fate of Plataea. Two are in the form of exhortations by commanders on the Athenian and Peloponnesian sides to their respective troops. The debate in the assembly over the invasion of Sicily in 415 entails three speeches: first Nicias, then Alcibiades, then Nicias again. A quartet of four speeches at Sparta in Book 1 is instrumental in laying out the national characters of the combatants, and the one conversation of any length, the dialogue on Melos, shines a very harsh light indeed on Athenian imperialism at its most glaringly naked.

Some speeches are conspicuous by their absence. We hear nothing of the heated debates that must have taken place in the Athenian assembly at two critical points. Perhaps the most important decision made by the Athenians in their history was the refusal to rescind the decree against Megara, a decision tantamount to voting for war with the Peloponnesian League. At that assembly, Thucydides says, 'Many people came forward to speak, and opinions were expressed on both sides—that war was called for, and that they repeal the decree and not let it stand in the way of preserving the peace.' But from all these many, the historian presents only a single speech: that of Pericles, arguing against repeal and for war.

Motivated at least in part by Thucydides' desire to create an alternative narrative in which Pericles did not bear responsibility for the ruinous war, the omissions concerning the decree(s) against Megara are the most startling in Thucydides' *History*. The sound reasons for peace presented by his opposition are nowhere included in his work, and all that remains is the bellicose speech of Pericles, as if that were the only possible approach to the conundrum. Pericles' role is downplayed in a different way in the follow-up to the first two speeches that Thucydides reproduces in his narrative, speeches that were no doubt exceptionally close to what was actually said, as the historian was surely in the assembly and heard them. When the Corcyraeans and Corinthians had both addressed the assembly in 433, Thucydides writes, the assembly met twice. At the first meeting, the inclination was to heed the words of the Corinthians. By the second, the Athenians had had a change of heart and voted to ally with Corcyra, but in a defensive alliance only; they would not join in any attack on Corinth.

Much like the debate over Megara, this was a pivotal moment in Athenian history, yet we hear nothing of the speeches it prompted in the assembly, for had he reproduced them, Thucydides would have had to acknowledge what Plutarch makes plain: Pericles changed people's minds. Here, in other words, Thucydides uses an opposite strategy from the one he deployed in the context of the Megarian debate, reproducing no speeches whatsoever.

The speeches of the Corcyraeans and Corinthians are the first of the many that dot Thucydides' narrative and are an integral part of it. The Corcyraeans emphasize expediency, whereas the Corinthians appeal to justice, hammering their argument home by using nearly 20 words with the stem for justice, *dik*-. Although the Corcyraeans do mention the virtue entailed in coming to the aid of an injured party against an aggressor, they also stress the good name the Athenians would earn from others and, most of all, the advantage that would accrue to Athens. Finally, they stress their value to the Athenians in the event of a war with the Peloponnesian League; and, they argue, any one of you who doubts that such a war is coming is kidding himself and fails to see that the Spartans, afraid of the Athenians' power, are eager for war. Corcyra, they point out, lies right on the route to Italy and Sicily and is in a position to prevent any fleet from reaching the Peloponnesus from the west, as well as block Peloponnesian ships from sailing the other way.

They save the most powerful argument for last. There are three navies of significance in the Greek world, they remind the assembly: those of Athens, Corcyra, and Corinth. If you stand by while Corinth absorbs our navy into its own, you will end up fighting against a formidable navy, whereas if you ally with us, you will be fighting with our ships as well as yours.

The Corinthian argument for justice is weak and consists primarily of character assassination heaped on dubious claims that an alliance with Corcyra would violate the terms of the Thirty Years Peace. The speakers paint the Corcyraeans as unsociable to the point of perversity, outside the recognized conventions of international civility, ascribing their previous neutrality to a positively criminal self-serving isolationism. Though the Corcyraeans may bill this neutrality as prudence, the truth is that they wanted no allies as witnesses to their crimes. No evidence is adduced for this claim, as there probably was none, but the speakers wisely call the Athenians' attention to the prospects for peace. It was Corinth, they insist, that dissuaded the Spartans from becoming involved in the Samian revolt, and in the Athenians' war with Aegina early in the 5th century the Corinthians had let them have 20 ships. So far, the implication is, relations between Athens and Corinth have not been so bad. The notion of an imminent war with which the Corcyraeans are trying to frighten the Athenians, moreover, was by no means a sure thing—although the alliance they were contemplating certainly risked making it a reality.

It was a tough call, perhaps the trickiest matter that had ever come before the Athenian assembly, yet we hear from Thucydides nothing of the debate that ensued. The paired speeches, however, serve as an effective introduction to the sorts of considerations the various states of Greece would be weighing throughout the war that followed. Thucydides brilliantly introduces us to the belligerents in that war by including in his narrative four of the speeches given at Sparta in 432 when the Spartans, no doubt under pressure from Corinth, took the unusual step of inviting anyone who wished to do so to address the Spartan assembly. The air was filled with tension, and Thucydides' dramatic presentation brings the scene vividly before our eyes. The format he chooses of four linked speeches—though plainly more were made—enables him to lay out the national character of the Athenians not in his own words but rather through the fiery rhetoric of the canny Corinthians, whose portrait of Athens, though bordering on caricature, events will show is not far off the mark.

The speech of the Corinthian ambassadors is a masterpiece of manipulation. In it the speakers recur again and again to the theme of Spartan cluelessness. The Spartans, they allege, have sat idly by while Athenian power grew steadily. They let the Athenians fortify their city after the Persian wars and later to erect the Long Walls that linked the city to its port. They fail, furthermore, to understand what makes the Athenians tick, or how great the struggle will be against a people so completely different from themselves. Consider this, they say:

> They are daring beyond their power and take risks beyond what makes sense . . . They are resolute where you procrastinate; they are never at home while you are never far from it, because they think that being abroad may pay off for them while you think that moving will endanger what you already have . . . Thanks to the speed with which they undertake whatever they have set their minds to, they are the only people in the world for whom achieving and hoping are virtually synonymous. . . . One would not go wrong to sum up by saying that they were born to take no rest themselves and grant none to anyone else either.

The Athenians, they warn, consider hard work a pleasure, the leisure that comes with peace and quiet practically a misfortune. As in their denigration of the Corcyraeans in their speech to the Athenian assembly, the Corinthians highlight character as a key issue, but here their purpose is different. Whereas in the Athenians they sought to instil dislike of the Corcyraeans, in the Spartans they aim to spark fear of the Athenians and, even more, insecurity about their own powers of discernment. And they conclude with a threat: do not let your allies down and drive us to seek alliance elsewhere. Coming from the supremely well-situated Corinth, with its substantial fleet, the threat to secede from the Peloponnesian League was a powerful one.

There 'happen' to be some Athenians present who ask to speak. This is no coincidence; plainly they had been sent at Pericles' behest. Their tone is forthright and unapologetic, and though their speech was probably not intended to provoke, apparently it did. Praising their conduct at Marathon and the role of the Athenian admiral Themistocles at Salamis, they point out that their post-war naval alliance fell to them by default when the Spartans let it go. It was not particularly remarkable or contrary to the customary practice of humankind, they say, to accept an empire that was offered to us and decline to give it up under the pressure of three of the strongest motives: fear, honour, and interest. And we were hardly the first to do this, for it has always been the law that the weaker should be subject to the stronger. Besides, we considered ourselves to be worthy of our position—as you also did until now when you have begun to confuse interest and justice.

If you were to take our place after defeating us in war, they add, it wouldn't be long before you lost all the good will you now enjoy from those who fear us. Deliberate slowly, then, bearing in mind the incalculable element in war, an element that grows incrementally the longer the fighting continues. So far nothing irrevocable has happened, and we are still free to resolve our differences by arbitration. They end on a religious note, reminding the Spartans that it is the gods who are guarantors of oaths—oaths such as the ones sworn at the end of the First Peloponnesian War agreeing to arbitration in the event of conflicts.

The next speaker is the Spartan king Archidamus, who is clearly alarmed by the mood he senses among his countrymen. *Not so fast,* he advises them, echoing the caution of the Athenian speakers. The Athenians are a formidable enemy, rich in ships and money. How will the landlubbing Spartans be able to defeat them with the Peloponnesian fleet in its current state? No matter how impressive its infantry, ultimately no power can bring Athens to its knees without a navy. This is a war that will drag on; so much so, he says, that we may find ourselves passing it on to our children. No, let us rather send embassies to negotiate with the Athenians now, and over a period of two—better still, three—years build up our strength, at which point we can, if we still want to, take on the Athenians from a more promising position. Our city follows a disciplined way of life that makes us both warlike and judicious. Raised in a tough school in accordance with the traditions of our ancestors, let us be sensible and take our time in deciding how to handle this situation. We live in a city, he says, renowned for its *sōphrosyne*: moderation, good sense, prudence.

The last speaker, the Spartan Sthenelaidas, shows the terseness associated with the English word *laconic*, which derives from the Spartans' territory of Laconia and originally means 'Spartan in speech'; he not only is succinct but sneers at the less economical presentation of the Athenians that has gone before. I can't follow all these words the Athenians have laid on us, he says. If they were good during the Persian wars but are bad now, they should be punished twofold for this decline. We, however, are the same now as ever, and we will not sit on our hands when our allies are being wronged. We may not have abundant ships and money, but we have worthy allies who must not be abandoned to Athenian aggression. Don't let anyone try to tell us that we should think things over for a while. Vote for war! Vote for Spartan honour! Do not, he concludes, 'allow the Athenians to grow even stronger. Rather than selling out our allies, let us with the gods on our side march out against these reprobates'! The Spartans responded by voting that the Athenians were in the wrong and had broken the truce, and at the meeting of the Peloponnesian League that followed, the allies voted to declare war.

Thucydides did not himself hear these speeches, and it is only reasonable to wonder whether the speakers were as prescient as he makes out. Did the Athenians really predict the unpopularity that would follow on a Spartan victory? Certainly the Spartans' bellicosity throughout the 4th century was profoundly alienating, so much so that it drove their key ally Thebes into the arms of the Athenians and prompted dozens of states to gather once again in an Athenian-led alliance. Did Archidamus really worry that the Spartans would pass this war on to their children, as they most certainly did? It would be nice to think that these forecasts were indeed made on this occasion, but the truth is that we can't be sure one way or the other.

Whatever the case, this quartet of speeches touches on themes that will persist throughout the *History*: the dynamics of national character, the value of deliberation, the laws that govern relations among states, the use of rhetoric to manipulate emotions, the dangers posed by hope and passion, the growth of Athens and the significance of naval power, the element of the incalculable in war, and not least the futility of reason in the face of strong emotion: both the full and careful presentation of the Athenians and the thoughtful, judicious eloquence of Archidamus are colossal failures.

The questions of justice and expediency raised in the paired speeches of the Corcyraeans and the Corinthians persist in a number of the paired speeches reproduced in Thucydides' text. Book 3 showcases the parallels between the situations of Plataea and Mytilene. In each case, one hegemon besieges a small state while the other side declines to intervene; food runs out, and a debate ensues in which the hegemon weighs the appropriate punishment—or, in the case of Plataea, pretends to. The debate over what to do with the rebellious city of Mytilene now that it has surrendered serves to introduce Cleon. He had been active in politics for some years, but Thucydides chooses to introduce him as the most violent man in the city at this juncture, crediting him with a speech in which he equates savagery with justice, sneers at the Athenian people, and denigrates deliberation—a speech that sets him up as not only the opposite of Pericles but, curiously, in some respects his heir as well.

Like the Corinthians at Sparta, he suggests that his hapless audience needs him to explain reality. Your behaviour, he begins, confirms my long-held belief that a democracy is incapable of running an empire. You have lost track of the fact, he says,

> that you hold your empire as a tyranny and that your subjects, who after all are governed unwillingly, are conspirators. Your suicidal concessions to them are not what is going to keep them in line; it's

the superiority you enjoy because of your strength, not their loyalty. The scariest thing of all is not sticking to your decisions and not realizing that bad laws that remain unchanged are better for a city than good ones that aren't enforced.

Having attacked democracy, he then goes on to denigrate the intellect, claiming that ignorance combined with prudence is far superior to quick-witted insubordination, and that ordinary men do a far better job in running cities than intelligent ones, since the smart ones are prone to considering themselves cleverer than the laws and are eager to pick holes in whatever speech they hear. Fine words and long deliberation, he argues, are a dangerous distraction. I, for one, am of the same opinion as before. Enough of this speechifying! The Mytileneans, full of hopes that exceeded their abilities, have done us grievous wrong and must be punished. What the Athenians need to do is get in touch with how angry they were when they passed the original decree and make clear to the world that the punishment for rebellion is death.

The echoes of earlier speakers come through loud and clear. Cleon follows Sthenelaidas in disparaging the value of speech, but the similarities to earlier remarks of Pericles—the empire is like a tyranny, I remain of the same opinion as always—are clear, and his tough stance on the empire evokes Pericles as well. Most intriguing of all is the fact that his presentation of his relationship to his audience is reminiscent of Thucydides himself, who also proclaims his intellectual superiority to the ordinary run of Athenians, those average people who believe everything they hear and are swept away by the pleasure that fine language affords the ear. Both lead off by disparaging their audience: Thucydides predicts that many people will be insufficiently curious about the truth to enjoy his work, and Cleon tells his listeners that they are idiots.

Cleon having couched his argument in terms of justice, the opposing speaker, the otherwise unknown Diodotus, grounds his own in expediency. If, as seems likely, he was motivated by compassion, he is shrewd enough not to let on. No matter how guilty the Mytileneans may be, he announces, he will not advise their execution unless it is to the advantage of the Athenians, just as no claims to indulgence could induce him to leniency unless it were clearly in Athens's interest. He begins by taking aim at Cleon's attack on deliberation and debate. The two things most opposed to good counsel, he says, are anger and haste. So much for Cleon's exhortation to the Athenians to get in touch with their initial rage. He follows this contention with the first documented argument against the deterrent value of punishment. People who commit crimes do so in the expectation that they will get away with it, and no threat of punishment however horrific seems to hold people back when they are egged on by hope. Think about it, he says. As things now stand, a rebellious city has a motive to surrender. Should we adopt Cleon's proposal, though, future rebels, having no such inducement, will hold out until the bitter end. We will be faced with costly sieges, the city we finally reduce will be in ruins—and we will lose what goodwill we have among our allies.

The vote was close, but the assembly chose to rescind the original decree.

In the second instance, that of Plataea, the matter of expediency is paramount, though largely unspoken. After a siege of two years, the Peloponnesian forces finally reduced Plataea to starvation. When the Plataeans agreed to surrender after the Spartans announced that the guilty among them would be punished 'but nobody treated unjustly', they must have been filled with both curiosity and terror. In the event, the Spartan judges put to them but a single question: had they done anything that would benefit the Spartans and their allies in the course of the war? The Plataeans' curiosity is now satisfied, their worst fears realized. They are doomed.

They nonetheless request the opportunity to respond at length, and the representatives whom they appoint to speak on their behalf make clear that they know that the Spartans have already made up their minds to destroy them as a favour to the Thebans. Nonetheless, they say, they will seek to change their minds by enumerating their services to Greece in times past: their loyalty during the Persian wars, in which the Thebans went over to Xerxes, and their contribution of a sizeable contingent to help the Spartans during the helot rebellion of 464. They appeal to Spartan interest as well, contending that while most Greeks considered the Spartans to be paragons of rectitude, that reputation would be lost should they destroy Plataea, a site revered as the final defeat of the Persian invasion in 479. 'Destroying our lives', they point out, 'is only a matter of a brief moment, but the struggle to erase the infamy you will bring on yourselves will be long and arduous.' Their speech was sufficiently moving to spark considerable anxiety in the Thebans, who then came forward and asked if they might speak before the Spartan judges announced their verdict. Their venomous response includes the doubtful claim that they had been under the unwelcome control of a narrow oligarchy, a tyrannical clique that hoped a Persian victory would entrench them in power. I cannot prove that this was not true, but supporting evidence has not come to light. Billing Athens as the new Persia, they suggest that the real traitors are the Plataeans, who allied with Athens in its aggression against the Greeks.

In fact, what the Plataeans and the Thebans have to say is of no consequence, for the Spartans have already decided to destroy the Plataeans lest they lose the goodwill of Thebes, whose superb infantry were crucial to the Peloponnesian military and who occupied a key location on the road to northern Greece. Thucydides' spare account leaves his distaste for the Spartans' actions in no doubt:

They once again had the Plataeans brought before them one by one and put to them the same question: had they ever done any service to the Spartans or their allies in the course of the war? When not a single one could answer yes, they were taken away and killed without exception, all 200 of them, along with 25 Athenians who had endured the siege with them. The women they sold as slaves. Virtually everything the Spartans did in abandoning the Plataeans to their fate was from a desire to please the Thebans, whom they considered useful in the war that was unfolding. Such was the end of the events at Plataea in the 93rd year after Plataea became an Athenian ally.

In this bare concluding sentence Thucydides' anger at his compatriots for their failure to help their long-standing ally is not far beneath the surface.

The themes that appeared in the speeches leading up to the war and during its earliest years will persist throughout Thucydides' *History*. Like the Athenian envoys at Sparta, the Sicilian Hermocrates cautions the Syracusans who want to resist the invading Athenians about the element of the unpredictability of war. The Athenians, the Corinthians said, considered rest positively oppressive, but Pericles tells the Athenians that they will succeed if they remain at rest and refrain from undertaking additional campaigns for the war's duration; Nicias in recommending that the Athenians reopen the question of attacking Sicily urges them to rest after the hardships of the war and the plague; and Alcibiades argues against too much rest, warning the Athenians that by remaining at rest they would never extend their empire; they might even lose it. Like Archidamus, Nicias advises caution, and like Diodotus, he praises the value of deliberation, but the Athenians' rejection of his eminently sound advice shows the futility of reason when emotion is running high.

Thucydides frames the opposing speeches of Nicias and Alcibiades to highlight the temperament of the Athenians, the dangers of emotion, and the deceptiveness of words. Nicias casts himself in the role of physician, aiming to heal a feverish assembly possessed by *erōs*, and his efforts fail conspicuously. A passion for the enterprise, Thucydides writes, fell on all alike, the older men feeling optimistic about the expedition's chances, the younger ones overcome with *pothos*: a powerful yearning after what is distant, what one does not have. Speaking in favour of the expedition, Alcibiades talks constantly about himself, drawing attention to his Olympic victories, the alliance he engineered between Athens and states in the Peloponnesus, and—the arduous battle at Mantinea, which the Athenians and their allies conspicuously lost! The Spartans, he concedes, were successful in the battle, but they have not to this day recovered their nerve: a barefaced lie, if we may believe Thucydides' assessment of the bounce-back in the Spartans' spirits following that battle.

He boasts, he lies. This is the kind of behaviour Thucydides had in mind when he wrote that the Athenians lost the war because they allowed private ambitions to lead them into projects 'harmful both to themselves and to their allies'. Ironically, Alcibiades devotes a good deal of his speech to the question of national character. The cities of Sicily, he argues,

> are populous only because they contain a mixed rabble in which people are constantly coming and going, with the result that there is no real civic feeling, no patriotism. Everyone strives after what he thinks he can obtain either by clever rhetoric or fomenting civil strife, with the idea in mind of fleeing the country if things don't work out according to plan.

The Sicilians, he maintains, are a ragtag bunch who couldn't possibly unite to form any successful resistance to the Athenians. Wrong! And they certainly couldn't muster enough of a fleet to do us any harm. Wrong again! It's almost too good to be true, isn't it, Alcibiades talking about people who think they can use fine language to obtain something at the public expense and then if something goes wrong decamp for another country? The speech perfectly encapsulates Alcibiades' narcissism and offers

detailed confirmation of Thucydides' earlier take on the loss
of the war arising from the replacement of the public
servant Pericles with self-centred politicians only interested in
their own well-being.

Is it true? Could Alcibiades really have said all this, thereby
condemning himself as precisely the sort of pernicious politician
who led to the loss of the war? Yes, but I would be lying if I said
I was confident that he did. As is always the case with speeches
in Thucydides' *History*, and most particularly in the case of
speeches Thucydides could not possibly have heard, the answer is
that we just don't know and are never likely to. And herein lies
a major conundrum, one that cannot be resolved and will continue
to nag at readers of Thucydides until they are just too exhausted to
think about it any further. Thucydides, we know, did not hear
Alcibiades' speech, and we know too that he used the speeches
that punctuate his *History* to elucidate his views of what really
motivated the participants in the war. But his views may have been
wrong, and where it comes to the speeches he reports in such
detail, this leaves us in a profoundly uncomfortable limbo from
which there is, alas, no escaping.

Chapter 7
Thucydides the political scientist

In using his history as a platform from which to analyse the workings of inter- and intra-state dynamics, Thucydides established himself as a premier political scientist (as we might term it today). Throughout his narrative he explored the subtle (and sometimes not so subtle) machinations of individuals, factions, and most of all states. He is probably most famous for his hard-headed analysis of international relations, but he was also interested in the internal workings of the Greek polis. The polis about which he knew, and cared, by far the most was his native Athens, and it is the Athenian democracy that receives his closest scrutiny.

We will never know the genesis of the speech Thucydides attributes to Pericles on the occasion of the funeral the Athenians held to honour those who died in the first year's fighting; it probably represents a mélange of Thucydidean and Periclean thinking. Plato may not have been joking when he ascribed it to Aspasia. Whatever its authorship, it is a passionate paean to the Athens of Pericles' day, albeit undercut by a number of ironies. He will, Pericles says, forgo a rehearsal of the city's string of glorious military victories and take rather as his subject the manner of government and way of life by which Athens has been brought to its present state.

Our government, he explains, is called a democracy because it is organized for the benefit of the many rather than the few. The speech as a whole, however, does not focus on democracy but on the Athenians' high level of culture and military might. We aspire to refinement, Pericles says, but without ostentation, and we cultivate knowledge without effeminacy. Regular festivals and games offer us the opportunity to return to toils with renewed energy. Pericles stresses the Athenians' relaxed approach to military training, contrasting it pointedly with the Spartans' system of relegating all males to barracks from an early age. The more easy-going Athenians, he boasts, are nonetheless every bit as successful in their military campaigns; they have compelled every land and every sea to yield to their daring as they established imperishable monuments to the vengeance they have taken on their enemies. If Athens has the greatest name in the world it is because she has ruled over more Greeks than any other Greek state and because the Athenians have expended more effort and life than any other city. In other words, *a higher proportion of Athenians have died in war than any other Greeks*. It is this for which Pericles envisioned Athens being remembered even should the vicissitudes of fortune someday lead it to fall, not the glorious buildings on the Acropolis or the magnificent tragedies performed annually at the festival of Dionysus. Forget *Antigone* and *Medea*; just focus on all those dead Athenian soldiers and sailors.

The contrast with Sparta is also implicit in Pericles' pointed observation that Athenians view public discourse as the best road to decision-making rather than a hindrance to action. Any Athenian man, he concludes, will prove more resilient and quick-witted and up to any challenge than anyone you would find elsewhere. As for Athenian women, he announced, the greatest virtue to which they could aspire was to be no worse than their natures, and to be least spoken of by men for either good or ill—this from a man whose life companion was more spoken of than any other woman in Athens.

Pericles' Athenians are versatile and cultivated, daring and vengeful. That Thucydides recreated Pericles' speech at length—some 3,000 words—strongly suggests his support for the Athens of Pericles' day, or at least of Pericles' imagining, but he was not blind to the speech's ironies. Pericles' claim that Athenians do not look askance at their neighbours if their habits give displeasure is not borne out by the evidence of Aristophanes or by the execution of Socrates a mere generation after Pericles' death or even by the way Thucydides himself presents the Athenians' treatment of Alcibiades, and the collapse of civic values during the plague that follows immediately in Thucydides' narrative offers a harsh corrective to Pericles' rosy picture of his countrymen's devotion to the community, not to mention their reverence for the law. Though easy-going in their private lives, Pericles claimed, Athenians had the greatest reverence for the laws, which they would not dream of breaking. This pointed reminder that the Spartans were not the only ones who stood in awe of their laws also rings hollow in retrospect when we consider the lawlessness that attended on the plague, when, Thucydides reported, people had no fear of breaking the law since nobody expected to live long enough to pay for their crimes.

Thucydides plainly saw the 30-year ascendancy of Pericles as an anomaly, as indeed it was; it was not the norm for Athenians to accord so much authority to an individual, and in fact the historian's view of democracy was a nuanced one. The portrait of the Athenians with which Thucydides credits the Corinthians when they sought to frighten the Spartans into war in 432 captured brilliantly the restless energy of the democracy, energy that Pericles alone had the capacity to harness in constructive ways. It was this same restlessness that would after Pericles' death lead the Athenians to undertake the disastrous expedition to Sicily that cost thousands of lives. Thucydides treats the Sicilian enterprise at such extraordinary length—two entire books—precisely because it represented for him the dangers that beset the volatile democracy when it was bereft of the calming influence of a leader of unquestioned authority, a man who combined foresight with eloquence and integrity. The supercharged state that the Corinthians billed as a danger to the Peloponnesian League was also a danger to itself.

The Athenians' susceptibility to high emotions concerned Thucydides a good deal. He construes Pericles' impeachment as a result of anger, and when the people then turned around and returned him to power, he characterizes their turnaround as 'the characteristic behaviour of the mob'. Most telling is his explanation of the impeachments of the three generals who returned from the first abortive expedition to Sicily in the 420s without accomplishing anything. Two were banished and the third fined. Because of the good fortune they had been experiencing, Thucydides wrote, the Athenians 'believed that they could achieve the possible and the impossible alike, regardless of how well or ill prepared they were'. They had been led to mistake their hopes for strengths, a propensity that the Corinthians had pegged as an asset but which is now revealed to be dangerous, a mindset that would deprive the Athenians of leaders like Thucydides, whose remarks on impeachments must be taken in the context of his own fate. Like anger, hope in Thucydides' view is an emotion that inhibits the judicious reasoning that makes for sound decision-making, and Thucydides made plain the dangers inherent in the emotions in which the Athenian voters often found themselves caught up.

Thucydides is also equivocal in his treatment of Sparta, the only other Greek state of which he offers any analysis; he seems to know nothing about the internal politics of Corinth. He takes care to present the two sides of Sparta, Archidamus representing the best and Sthenelaidas the worst. The judicious Archidamus praised the Spartans for their *sōphrosyne*, a quality on which Greeks placed enormous value. It derives from *sōphrōn*, wise, prudent, and in fact Thucydides describes Archidamus himself as *sōphrōn*, the only individual in the *History* to whom he accorded this honour. Because of their moderation, the king said, the Spartans do not give way to *hybris* when events turn out well. Conspicuously, Thucydides never attributes *sōphrosyne* to the Athenians, and he would certainly have been the first to agree that success did in fact lead the Athenians into *hybris*. Archidamus' fellow Spartans, however, rejected his counsel by opting for war, just as the Athenians ultimately rejected that of Pericles by marching out to meet the Peloponnesians on land and by undertaking expeditions far from home. The absence of reasoned discussion may well have played a role in the Spartans' vacillating policy in the run-up to the war. Sthenelaidas' crude appeal to the least productive of emotions leads to what amounted to a declaration of war, but the Spartans then immediately turn around and look for ways out of it. In Pericles' absence, however, it was the very presence of discussion in the Athenian assembly that came increasingly to evoke dangerous emotions. Cleon came within a hair's breadth of getting the Athenians to obliterate Mytilene, and Alcibiades succeeded in implanting in his audience *erōs* for the ruinous expedition to Sicily.

Altogether Thucydides' treatment of Athens's great foe is mixed. To recover the men stranded on Sphacteria Island, the Spartans offer the Athenians not only peace but alliance. This, they argue, is the time to make peace before something irreversible should happen resulting in irremediable hatred (presumably the capture and killing of the Spartans on Sphacteria), and once we are seen to be united, we will command respect from all Greece. Of course, this move is born of desperation; the loss of the hoplites on the island would be both a humiliation and a serious diminution of manpower. Still, nowhere in the text of Thucydides do we hear Athenians speaking like this.

In the end, Thucydides endorses neither the democracy of his native city nor the peculiar mixed government of its rival. When the narrow oligarchy that had seized power in Athens after the Sicilian debacle had been replaced with a larger group composed of all who could afford hoplite armour, Thucydides observed that the Athenians in the early days of this constitution enjoyed the best government they ever had in his lifetime, with its blend of oligarchic and democratic elements. This certainly tells us something about Thucydides' political orientation, for the poor were entirely excluded. This body, however, governed for only a few months before the democracy was restored, and Thucydides' claim raises questions concerning the ascendancy of Pericles about which he had been so enthusiastic, for Pericles was elected in significant part by poor men disfranchised under the oligarchy. It may be that Thucydides placed more faith in good leaders than in good constitutions: Pericles and Archidamus are presented in a far better light than the systems that brought them to power.

It is striking that a man of Thucydides' social class, plainly disturbed by the direction Athenian politics took during the war, did not place the blame for Athens's misfortunes primarily on the democratic principle that granted equal political power (in theory, at least) to rich and poor, educated landowners and unschooled day labourers. What troubled him about the democracy was principally the rivalries it engendered among aspiring politicians, many of whom were in fact aristocrats from his own class, and the play it gave to rhetoric and to the emotions it evoked. Democracy can give rise to a statesman like Pericles but it also has room for a crude Cleon, a vacillating Nicias, and a self-interested Alcibiades. Ultimately, however, the value Thucydides placed on reasoned deliberation—a process that inevitably entailed rhetoric—tilted the balance towards Athens. While he was all too aware of the pitfalls of rhetoric, in the end talking is better than not talking, and the canards lobbed at fancy language by Sthenelaidas and Cleon undermine the speakers.

Along with Pericles' funeral oration, the dialogue Thucydides ascribes to representatives from Athens and Melos in 415 is the segment of the *History* that is most frequently assigned to students. Wrongly taken to embody Thucydides' ideas about foreign policy in their entirety, it needs rather to be understood in the broader context of Thucydides' *History* as well as the deeper context of Greek thought.

For reasons unknown to us, in 416 the Athenians resolved to bring the neutral little island of Melos into their empire. A Spartan colony, Melos was the only island in the Cyclades that had remained aloof from the Delian League, and the Athenian commanders on their arrival propose a parley with the Melian leadership, to which the Melians agree. The Athenians begin ominously by announcing that questions of justice are to be excluded from the conversation, as justice, after all, is a meaningful consideration only among equals. The powerful, they say, do what they can while the weak have no choice but to accommodate them. The Melians make the excellent point that should the Athenians mistreat them they would be setting an example for all states that hold power, something that would come back to haunt them should they lose the war, but the underwhelmed Athenians profess not to be concerned about this prospect.

The Melians put forward three reasons for declining to submit to the Athenians: Spartan aid; divine support; and hope. The Athenians quickly dismiss the prospect of Spartan assistance, pointing out that the Spartans have never been known as big risk-takers, and Athens after all controls the seas. So far, so good, but the speakers bring disgrace on themselves by comparing themselves to the very gods on whom the Melians are counting. They are not worried, they say, about divine intervention standing in their way. When it comes to divine favour, they say,

> we don't anticipate being left out. We're not doing or demanding anything contrary to what people think about the gods or their behaviour. Of the gods we believe, and of people we know, that a necessary law of nature compels them to dominate wherever they

can. It's not as if we were the first to make use of this law: it existed long before us, and we will leave it to exist for eternity after us, knowing perfectly well that you or anyone else would do the same thing if they had the power that we do. So as far as the gods are concerned, it's not likely we need to fear any disadvantage.

In other words, we are hardly the first to behave like this. Don't you understand that has always been the way of the world?

As for hope, it is important to remember that the Greeks did not regard it at all as favourably as many are prone to do today. In the United States, for example, where I live, much has been made of hope by the Democratic Party, which capitalized on the fact that presidential candidate Bill Clinton hailed from the town of Hope, Arkansas; during the 2007–8 presidential campaign, artist Shepard Fairey designed a poster featuring Barack Obama and the word HOPE in large block sans serif capitals. Greeks viewed hope differently: the twin of danger, the Megarian poet Theognis called it, 'spirits of evil both'. Close cousin to delusion, hope led people to imagine they could determine the future by wishing for it. Thucydides makes plain his own view of hope in discussing the decision of the cities near Amphipolis to revolt to Brasidas following its fall. Their failure to estimate the Athenians' power correctly, he maintained, was based on wishful thinking rather than sound reasoning, for 'when they long for something, people are accustomed to placing themselves in the hands of unconsidered hope'.

The men who would soon resolve to sail to Sicily over the sensible reservations of Nicias have some nerve cautioning the Melians against vain hopes. When *erōs*, Thucydides says, overcame the Athenians for the Sicilian enterprise, those in their prime were of good hope that they would be safe. We know what became of that hope. In their characterization of the Athenians at Sparta, the Corinthians had painted them as hopeful even in the direst straits. As so often, the Athenians' behaviour with regard to the expedition to Sicily confirms the accuracy of the Corinthians' perception. But the Corinthians also said that for the Athenians hoping for something and achieving it were synonymous, and in this instance they were profoundly mistaken. Like the Melians, the Athenians are sorely, fatally disappointed in their hopes. Since Thucydides plainly fell behind in his plan of writing up each year as it happened, when he was laying out the dialogue on Melos, he was well aware of the debacle to which the Athenians' hopes would soon egg them on, a fact that casts still further shade on the Athenians' position, already alienating in its amalgam of amorality and condescension.

Thucydides' readers were well educated. Books were hard to come by in Greece, and few people had developed the habit of plodding through long, challenging texts. It is safe to assume that the pool of individuals who had the education and the leisure to curl up with Thucydides' challenging narrative overlapped considerably with those who were familiar with Herodotus' work, and readers of Herodotus would instantly have been reminded of a parallel discussion he reproduced between the Athenians and an emissary proposing submission to Persia. Some Athenians might also have heard about this event from their ancestors. The Athenians, Herodotus reported (and of course we cannot know exactly what they really said), replied that it was pointless to remind them how much greater the power of Persia was than their own, because they valued their liberty too much to give it up. Tell Xerxes' general, they say, that as long as the sun rises and sets we will never accept his terms. Rather, we will fight against him unceasingly, trusting in the aid of the gods whom he has disrespected, burning their temples and images to the ground. They assure the Spartans that many factors stand in the way of their ever coming to an accommodation with Xerxes, adducing the common way of life the Greeks share, the shared shrines and sacrifices, the kinship of all Greeks in blood and speech. All this is summed up in the phrase *to hellenikon*: Greekness.

Not only did the Athenians refuse to accept the inevitability of bowing to *force majeure*, but they did so by appealing to the unity of all the Greeks, precisely what they have now set about to destroy. Their rationale for their empire was never the unity of the Greeks but rather the security of the Greeks against the Persians—and subsequently the security of the Athenians against their own subject allies. As for the gods, the very Athenians whose grandsons would scoff at the Melians' faith in divine aid had not long before vowed to fight against a vastly superior power trusting in their gods. A look back at their risky resistance to the Persians, moreover, makes their derision of the Melians' suicidal recklessness particularly distasteful.

The Melian dialogue is the mirror image of the debate at Plataea. At Plataea it was the Spartans who killed indiscriminately after a debate that was not a debate, whereas now it is the Athenians who kill all the men they can get their hands on after a dialogue that is not a dialogue; in both instances, the parties were talking past one another, and no actual communication took place. The Athenians often boasted of the *parrhesia* they enjoyed in their democracy: frank speech. Their speech at Melos is nothing if not frank.

Thucydides was far from the first to articulate the pitiless view of power relations that he puts in the mouths of Athenians, first at Sparta on the eve of the war and subsequently at Melos. The formative poets of Greek civilization had portrayed characters pointing out the futility of resisting *force majeure* two or three centuries before. The context of these observations, however, makes clear a dramatic difference in their thinking. Homer's contemporary Hesiod bequeathed to the Greeks a remarkable work chock full of ethical maxims as well as advice on farming, the *Works and Days*. The poem took the form of an address to Hesiod's brother Perses, who had bribed the local magistrates to award him the better share of the land the two brothers had inherited. Buried in the long poem is a fable about the hawk and the hapless nightingale it had seized in its talons—a tale, the poet says, that is addressed specifically to rulers. In response to the bird's piteous cries, he recounts, the hawk said:

> Bird, why do you howl? The one who now holds you fast
> Is far stronger than you, and lovely as is your song,
> Where I go, you must go also, and it is up to me
> Whether to eat you or not. He is a fool pure and simple
> Who tries to withstand the stronger. Not only does he lose,
> But he compounds his shame with pain.

So spoke the hawk; but you, Perses, the poet continues, returning now to address his errant brother,

> Pay heed to what is just and do not foster hybris.

Rather, he says, follow the road of justice, for in the end justice will best hybris. The entire city suffers when the government is corrupt, but when rulers govern fairly, the city will prosper; Zeus keeps war away, the earth bears plentiful crops, and altogether the people flourish.

Hesiod, then, decisively rejects the ideology of the hawk. It may be the law of the jungle, but it is not how humans should live; it is not in keeping with the design of Zeus. Rulers can accept bribes, but they can also decide to heed Hesiod's words and decline them. Around the same time, Homer engaged a similar question in the *Iliad*. In one of the many excruciatingly painful battlefield scenes that dot the poem, the Trojan prince Lycaon begs Achilles to spare his life. His entreaty fails utterly. There is no chance I will let you go, Achilles tells him, and he not only kills Lycaon and throws him into the river but gloats in telling him that his family will never be able to hold a funeral for him; rather the fish will eat the fat from his bones, and not even the god of the river will be of any use to him, although no doubt he has sacrificed many large animals in his honour. Lycaon must yield not only his life but

his burial to the stronger, and as will be the case with
the Melians, piety avails him naught; the river god does not
come to his aid.

Achilles' awareness of his own vulnerability makes a strong
contrast with the Athenians at Melos, who scoff at the Melians'
suggestion that they think twice about exterminating them
since it would set a bad precedent for the day when some
other state (think Sparta) has worsted them in war; they
dismiss this notion out of hand. Achilles has a sounder grasp
of the parameters governing human existence. Are you so
special, he asks Lycaon? Look at me, how handsome I am,
and what illustrious parents brought me into being. Why, my
mother was a goddess! Yet death hangs over me just as it does
over everyone else:

> There will come a time, whether it be in the morning or evening,
> Or perhaps in the middle of the day, when some soldier will take my life
> Perhaps with the cast of his spear, perhaps with the tang of his bow.

This humility makes a sharp contrast to the Athenians' smug
self-assurance. It is a great loss that we do not have Thucydides'
account of the war's end; it was left to his continuator Xenophon
to tell how when the news of the disaster at Aegospotami
arrived at Athens the citizens could not sleep a wink, as they
mourned not only the men who had died in the battle but far more
for themselves, believing that they would suffer the same
treatment they had meted out to the people of Melos and many
other Greek cities. No doubt at least a few of the men who had
rounded up the Melians and put them to the sword were among
the petrified insomniacs.

The era of the Peloponnesian War was also the great age of the
Sophists. Plato's dislike of Sophists is evident throughout his
work. To their emphasis on rhetoric and relativism he opposed the
search for absolute truth. Nonetheless, his portrayal of sophistic

reasoning may not have been entirely incorrect. Both Thrasymachus (a real Sophist) in the *Republic* and Callicles (possibly fictional) in *Gorgias* give some sense of what Sophists had to say about power relations both within the polis and among states. Justice, Thrasymachus maintained, is very simply the advantage of the stronger party; nature itself, Callicles announced, has proclaimed that it is just for the stronger to rule over the weaker, and he adduces as evidence the most provocative example possible. In marching on Greece, he claims, Xerxes was doing nothing but following the nature of the just, and he mocks Socrates for failing to accept this plain truth. Clearly such ideas were current in the war years, when Thucydides was writing and Socrates was engaging in conversation with young men who held views like these.

Unlike Hesiod and Plato, Thucydides does not distance himself from his speakers' articulation of an ethic of power; unlike Homer, he does not show his speakers' awareness that they too are mortals and hence subject to the very fate they are doling out. His own awareness, however, is manifest in his treatment of the unsuccessful expedition to Sicily that followed. The Athenians on Melos denied that they would reap what they had sown, but they were mistaken, not because of the kind of cosmic balancing evident in Herodotus' narrative but because the dangers they had identified lurking in hope were all too real.

The patron saint of political realism, Thucydides was the first to analyse balance of power politics, or at least the first to leave a record of his analysis. His picture of international relations in many ways corresponds to that of realists today. When on the eve of the war the Athenian envoys lay before the Spartans their position on their empire, they mince no words. After all, they maintain, the Spartans had used their supremacy in the Peloponnesus to their own advantage, for that is how people behave. If they and not the Athenians had gained empire over the other Greeks, they would no doubt also have become every bit as galling to their subjects and would have been forced, as the Athenians had been, to protect themselves by governing with an iron hand. It follows, they conclude, that

> we did nothing out of the ordinary in accepting the empire that was offered to us and declining to give it up, acting as we did under the compulsion of three of the most powerful motives there are: fear, honour, and self-interest. And we were not the first to behave in this way, for it has always been the law that the strong should rule over the weak.

This statement has since become known as 'the Athenian thesis'. Thucydides himself, however, was acutely sensitive to the complexity of human motivation. He was aware that the causes of the war he set out to document were multifarious, as witness his statement that the growth of Athens and the fear it inspired in Sparta was the truest cause of the war, the *alethestate prophasis*. Where there is a truest cause, there are plainly additional causes to be taken into consideration, causes that while not false are nonetheless not quite as central. His interest in both individual and national character makes clear that he ascribed the course of history to a wide variety of factors.

The civil strife that racked Greece throughout the war, Thucydides observed, 'opened the door to every form of iniquity imaginable, and the old-fashioned guilelessness, to which high-minded nobility was central, was laughed down and vanished'. But Thucydides' own persistent concern with matters of fairness makes clear that this high-mindedness had by no means entirely disappeared. The stasis in Corcyra and elsewhere plainly caused him tremendous pain, and he was appalled by the behaviour of the Spartans at Plataea and the Athenians at Melos. He can hardly have been the only Greek alive who felt this way.

It is easy to imagine that the individuals whose uncompromising speeches Thucydides records spoke for all, but that was not the case. Sparta sent envoys to Delphi to explore the advisability of the war even after the assembly had voted that the truce had been broken. It took the eloquence of a Pericles to dissuade the Athenians from making the concessions that would have avoided war. Some Athenians voted with Cleon about Mytilene, but somewhat more supported Diodotus' motion, and the ship sent out to report the Athenians' change of heart was able to overtake the earlier one since the first crew 'was in no great hurry to perform its distasteful duty'. We have no idea how many Athenians were comfortable with the party line promulgated at Sparta in 432 and Melos in 416. The weak, say the Athenians, must yield to the strong; that is just the way things are, have always been, and always will be. Not so. The bodies of the dead Melians make clear that the weak are not in fact compelled to yield to the strong; they can choose to die.

Appealing to his contention that the war resulted from the Spartans' alarm at the growth in the power of Athens, modern realists hail Thucydides as the first to explore the notion of balance of power and to analyse the problems that arise from shifts in that balance. Thucydides, however, placed too much weight on the idiosyncrasies of individual statesmen to be a pure realist, and the Greek preoccupation with honour also militated against any simplistic model of foreign relations. Political actors make free choices, as do the Melians, who might well have chosen differently. Thucydides makes plain that not all individuals respond in the same way in a given situation. While I would certainly stop short of labelling Thucydides an optimist, I wonder if his pessimism has not been exaggerated. Plainly a labour of love, his *History*, meant, as he said, to be 'a possession for all time', would have had little point had he really believed that a healthy state of domestic and international affairs was really unattainable—that his readers could never change, never learn.

The grim inevitability of historical processes is key to modern realist theory, but despite Thucydides' much-quoted contention that the Spartans' fear of Athens' growing power forced them into war, close attention to the text suggests that Thucydides did not always think of the war as inevitable. While a shift in the balance of power certainly played an important role, the deliberations in Sparta make clear that the Spartans who voted for war did not in fact fear the Athenians. The followers of Archidamus plainly did, but it was not their faction that triumphed. Rather, the decision for war was made by those who, like Sthenelaidas, were motivated by resentment and the need to preserve Sparta's reputation. Modern realists claim a unique superiority for their own vision, billing those who see the world differently as not merely mistaken but embarrassingly naive. This attitude is absent from the text of Thucydides, who takes no satisfaction in the cold light he shines on the self-interest that guides political actors; rather he makes plain the biting sorrow it causes him. Rich and complex, both ambivalent and multivalent, the *History* offers no simple schemata that can explain anything as problematic as human behaviour.

In Thucydides' account, the war arises from a chain of events any of which might have gone the other way: the Corcyraean rebuff of the Epidamnians, the Corinthians' choice to help them, the hard-debated Athenian vote to ally with Corcyra, the Athenians' decision to enact the decree against Megara and to stick by it despite the threat of war. Athenian power had not in fact increased since the end of the First Peloponnesian War; the Athenians made no new conquests and added no new allies to the empire. As for Melos, Thucydides had no need to reconstruct the episode as he did. He might well have treated it quite differently, writing:

> That summer the Athenians sent a force of 38 ships against the island of Melos, a colony of Sparta that stood out from the other islanders in its refusal to submit to Athenian control. Hoping to avoid military action, the generals sent ambassadors to urge the

Melians to join the empire, but when their efforts failed, they reduced the island to subjection, killing what men they could get their hands on and enslaving the women and children.

He opted instead to highlight the episode by recounting it in detail and reconstructing an elaborate conversation that he had never heard. He has opted to underscore the happenings on Melos just as he chose to include the militarily inconsequential attack of the Thracian mercenaries on little Mycalessus. The messages are similar: war is hell. Here, however, the villains—and they are certainly painted as villains—are not crude foreigners (Thracians on a rampage, Thucydides wrote of the massacre at Mycalessus, are a murderous lot) but cultivated Athenians who have plainly learned from the Sophists. In assessing the proclivity of 5th-century Athenians to place greed and power above human decency, we must remember that Thucydides, son of Olorus, was himself a 5th-century Athenian.

Chapter 8
Thucydides' legacy

Like any classic, Thucydides' narrative invites readers into a dialogue that transcends generations. The historian's hope that his history would be of enduring value has plainly been realized. Selections are regularly assigned to students, and journalists frequently appeal to his wisdom to bolster their arguments. From monarchists to republicans to neoconservatives, readers of Thucydides—including many who have read him only selectively—have proudly cited his work in defence of their ideologies. He has been brought forward as both a strategist for war and a pacifist. Indeed, his text has served as something of a Rorschach test, as all who examine it seem to find that Thucydides foreshadowed their own thinking quite precisely. Time and again Thucydides' readers were convinced that he was talking directly to them. John Adams spoke for many when he observed in a letter to Thomas Jefferson that when reading Thucydides, 'I seem to be only reading the History of my own Times and my own Life.'

Inevitably, those who had lived through the Peloponnesian War engaged with Thucydides' text. Xenophon and several others continued his narrative, and a variation on Pericles' funeral speech appeared around 387 in Plato's dialogue *Menexenus*, where Plato issued a broadside against Pericles' amoral framework for praising the city. The alternative speech Socrates delivers undermines that of Pericles at every turn, praising justice and virtue rather than military success and versatility. As time passed, however, the *History* received limited attention. Thucydides had boasted that entertainment was not his goal, and, sure enough, readers in the centuries that immediately followed his death gravitated to the more amiable Herodotus and Xenophon. In this he paid the price for the convoluted, sometimes tortuous prose style that resulted in a demanding narrative less pleasing and more taxing than theirs. Some found his adamantly secular perspective distasteful, and many found his subject matter problematic. Where the struggle with Persia had been inspirational, the Peloponnesian War was downright depressing.

The following centuries witnessed a burst of interest in Thucydides, but interest is not the same as admiration. The historian and rhetorician Dionysius of Halicarnassus condemned Thucydides' choice of subject matter: 'an inglorious war with a dreadful outcome that should never have happened at all, or should at the very least been forgotten by subsequent generations, consigned to silence and oblivion'. The first task of a historian, Dionysius proclaimed, was to select a subject that was noble and pleasing. Where Herodotus had shown pleasure at the good and distress at the bad, Thucydides, bearing a grudge against Athens because of his exile, went into minute detail about all the city's mistakes. Not only will those who focus historical narratives on deeds inglorious or evil forgo the admiration of posterity, Dionysius contended, but indeed readers will conclude that the authors' own lives were equally depraved.

Convinced that hostility to his countrymen lay behind the section of Thucydides' narrative that most distressed him, the Melian dialogue, Dionysius is quick to accuse Thucydides of bias against the men who exiled him. He was apoplectic in denying that Athenians could ever have let such tyrannical and blasphemous words escape their lips. Would it not be horrendous, after they had led the Greeks to victory over the Persian Empire, for them to tell the Melians that there is no point in a weaker power resisting a far stronger one? It would indeed, but this is not to say it did not happen. Dionysius finds it still more unthinkable that the Athenians would have derided the Melians' trust in prophecies, oracles, and gods. If there is one thing we know of the Athenians, he maintains, it is that they followed divine guidance at every turn, taking no important action without consulting oracles and seers. No, it is simply not possible that the Athenians should have spoken as Thucydides said they did.

In Rome, however, Thucydides found an admirer, indeed an emulator. Rome's defeat of the Macedonian king Perseus in 168 had dramatic consequences for the evolution of Roman civilization, for in its wake Rome was flooded by a torrent of Greek books, Greek works of art, and Greek people. Thucydides may have spent part of his exile in the Macedonian capital of Pella, and certainly copies of his work would have been in the library there. Some of the Greeks who now found themselves in Rome were slaves and spent the remainder of their lives as tutors to elite Roman children, but a thousand of them were high-ranking men brought to Rome as hostages, and among these was the historian Polybius. Polybius developed great admiration for Rome and devoted himself to writing a history of its rise in which he scrutinized the outlook and institutions that explained its success. Predictably, his analytical mindset drew him to the writing of Thucydides.

At the outset of his work Thucydides had taken care to distinguish between the *aitiai*, the specific disputes that triggered the Peloponnesian War, and the underlying cause, *prophasis*, which he identified as the Spartans' fear of Athens's growing power. Polybius, in discussing the Punic Wars between Rome and Carthage, plainly sought to refine Thucydides' formulation. In a passage that makes use of precisely the same key words as had appeared in Thucydides' text—*aitiai, prophasis*—he puts forward a very different scheme. Some, he complains, are not capable of understanding the difference between a cause and a pretext, but he himself will seek causes, *aitiai*, in the motives that prompted the actions. He plainly had Thucydides' text in mind when he wrote that historical analysis such as that which he aims to supply will be useful to future readers in a way that a merely entertaining narrative will not. 'If you remove from history all explanation of such things as causes, principles, and motives', he declared, 'all you have left is a panorama of no educational value—something that, though it may give pleasure in the moment, has no use whatsoever as a guide to the future.'

Another influx of Greek books followed the sack of Athens in 86 by the future dictator Sulla, and by the middle of the 1st century numerous Roman writers showed familiarity with Thucydides' work. The poet Lucretius followed Thucydides closely in describing the plague at Athens, some lines reading virtually as translations from the Greek, and Cicero in discussing Greek oratory betrayed the assumption that the speeches in Thucydides' narrative were in fact composed verbatim by their speakers rather than by the application of Thucydides' intellect to what material he had at hand. The most dramatic instance of Thucydidean influence can be found in the work of Julius Caesar's contemporary Sallust, labelled two generations later by the historian Velleius Paterculus *aemulus Thucydidis*, Thucydides' rival. The two historians were linked by their obvious pain at what they saw as the decline of their respective civilizations, and like Thucydides Sallust wrote about it in a style that was concise, compressed, and trenchant.

Sallust lays out at the beginning of his history of Catiline's conspiracy the collapse in character and morals that he perceives as having overtaken his countrymen. When Roman power had increased by the overthrow of foreign powers, he wrote, most dramatically Carthage, those who had readily endured all manner of danger now replaced patriotism with avarice and ambition. Deceit took over, and people came to keep one thing hidden in the breast but another ready on the tongue. Like Thucydides, Sallust employed speeches as a means of political analysis, and when Sallust's Cato laments that the Romans 'have lost the true names for things; now lavishing what belongs to others is labelled generosity, and audacity in wickedness is called bravery', we hear a clear echo of Thucydides' observations on the civil war in Corcyra, where daring impervious to reason was viewed as courage and plotting against someone without getting caught was the height of cleverness.

Helped along by the many people enslaved in Rome's eastern wars and transported to the capital, the ability to read Greek was common in the Roman elite, where study of Thucydides persisted for centuries and continued when the centre of power shifted to Byzantium. When the fall of Byzantium to the Ottoman Turks in 1453 sent Greek scholars scurrying westward, Hellenic studies, largely neglected during the European Middle Ages, came to the fore once again, and the question arose who would translate Thucydides into the languages of the West. When such a project was proposed to Leonardo Bruni in 1407 by his fellow humanist Niccolo Niccoli, Bruni recoiled in horror. How many sleepless nights, he exclaimed, such a project would entail! Translations of Thucydides began nearly half a century later with Lorenzo Valla's 1452 Latin edition, commissioned by Pope Nicholas V. Other renditions followed, though Claude de Seyssel derived his French version from Valla's translation rather than directly from the Greek, and Thomas Nicolls based his English version on Seyssel's French one; the first translation of Thucydides into a modern language made directly from the Greek was that published in 1629 by Thomas Hobbes. Thucydides can now be read in dozens of languages on every continent.

For many generations, Thucydides suffered particularly in comparison with the more charming Plutarch, whose biographies were replete with edifying moral exempla. In time, however, Thucydides came to be cherished as an authority par excellence to whom one could appeal to buttress any political position whatsoever as one generation after another has convinced itself that he was speaking, above all, to them. Thucydides served early modern Europe as an authority one could cite with profit in championing pre-emptive war: do unto others, his admirers cautioned, before they do unto you! Oxford law professor Alberico Gentili (1555–1608) in advocating such campaigns cited the words of the Mytileneans in defending their rebellion: since the Athenians always had the opportunity of harming them, they explain, they ought to have the privilege of anticipating such wrongs, and he goes on to enquire how one might go about deciding among thinkers who disagree about this. Should we not, he asks, side with that illustrious and sagacious man Thucydides?

In taking issue with Gentili, the eminent Dutch scholar Hugo Grotius (1583–1645) quoted at length from the Corinthians' speech at Sparta. There, he maintained, Thucydides suggested that only an injury justifies the declaration of war. He also cites Thucydides in defence of the argument that one party may proceed to war only if arbitration is declined by the other. In deciding on war, he claimed, the Spartans were in the wrong; fear of a neighbouring power is insufficient cause unless it is virtually certain that such a power intends to attack. Francis Bacon (1561–1626) cited the identical passage, however, in defence of the Spartan decision. Thucydides, he points out, did not hesitate to call it '*A necessity imposed upon the [Spartans] of a Warre*: Which are the Words of a mere Defensiue: Adding, that the other Causes were but specious and Popular'. From this Bacon concluded that as it was a fundamental law in the Turkish Empire that it was free to make war upon Christendom without provocation, therefore the Christians, living as they did in perpetual fear, were free at all times to attack them pre-emptively.

Justus Lipsius (1547–1606) in his 1589 *Politica* cited Thucydides as an authority over 30 times, appealing to the speeches of Cleon to buttress his arguments against popular rule. Presumably Cleon too was in his mind when he wrote that maintaining the same laws, even if they are bad, is superior to changing them. The influence of the *Politica* was immense. Within 10 years of its publication it appeared in 10 editions, and by 1604 it had been translated into seven languages.

Opponents of democracy like Hobbes in the 17th century and French philosopher Gabriel Bonnot de Mably in the 18th heard Thucydides decrying its inherent foolishness. Writing shortly before 1800, Thucydides' French translator Pierre Lévesque expressed confidence that what was to be learned from Thucydides was the futility of small republics and the superiority of the sort of stable monarchical rule found in Macedon. In Britain, William Mitford, the late 18th-century historian of Greece, saw in Thucydides' account of Athenian imperialism a clear parallel to French expansionism. In 1835 Thomas Arnold in the preface to the third volume of his edition of Thucydides proclaimed that 'the history of Greece and Rome is not an idle inquiry about remote ages and forgotten institutions, but a living picture of things present, fitted not so much for the curiosity of the scholar as for the instruction of the statesman and the citizen'. Arnold's words seemed so apt that they were deployed as the epigram for the collection of Edward Freeman's *Historical Essays* that appeared a half-century later in 1873 and again by Sir Thomas Erskine May in his 1877 *Democracy in Europe*.

While some in Victorian Britain argued that there was nothing to be learned from the study of a pagan slave-owning society whose economy was grounded primarily in agriculture, others disagreed. Utilitarian philosopher John Stuart Mill believed that much could be learned from a study of Athens, and his Athens was very much the Athens of Thucydides' narrative—but with his own view of what Athens should ideally have had grafted upon it. The happy Athens Mill inferred from his reading of Thucydides succeeded because it placed political power in the hands of men from the 'instructed classes' like Nicias, Alcibiades, and most of all

Pericles, the deployment of Cleon at Pylos and Amphipolis being merely exceptions to the rule—surely an extraordinary reading given that the collapse of Athens was due certainly to Nicias and Alcibiades and quite possibly to Pericles as well.

Thomas Arnold's son Matthew deemed 5th-century Athens far more modern than Elizabethan England and consequently its study more useful to his own age. In the Athens of Pericles, he inferred from the funeral oration, there was toleration; not so in 16th-century England, when the Puritans flourished. Put off by chapter titles like 'Of Fate, and that the stars have great influence', he compared Sir Walter Ralegh's *History of the World* invidiously with Thucydides' more rigorously critical narrative. Altogether, he suggested, his contemporaries should aspire to become more Greek.

Statesmen as well as intellectuals have considered Thucydides' work a repository of priceless instruction. In the 15th century Alfonso the Magnanimous, king of Aragon, was said to have copied Thucydides' text frequently by his own hand, and the 16th-century Holy Roman Emperor and king of Spain Charles V apparently carried a copy of Thucydides with him while on campaign. A distinguished 18th-century English member of Parliament claimed there was no question with which he was compelled to deal in debate on which Thucydides did not afford guidance. Across the Atlantic, John Adams viewed Thucydides' text differently. Contemplating the horrors of the Peloponnesian War, he remarked that Thucydides' belief that 'such things will ever be . . . as long as human nature continues the same' arose from his unfamiliarity with 'the salvation that would come from the concept of a balance of powers'. Still, America's founders considered Thucydides' work well worth reading: Adams himself advised his son, the future president John Quincy Adams, to read Thucydides in the original, and Thomas Jefferson reported in his retirement that when he was not playing with his grandchildren he was reading Thucydides.

Thucydides had described the Peloponnesian War as a cataclysm that shook the whole world around him, and many found the horrors of the First World War unnervingly similar. Soldiers in the trenches wrote of thinking about Thucydides in their dark hours, even of reading his text. The trauma of the war had the effect of converting Thucydides' text from a source for 5th-century Athens to an exposition of the human condition and the concomitant rise and fall of civilizations. It was this war that turned the attention of the Briton Arnold Toynbee—a historian so prominent that he was declared *Time* magazine's man of the year in 1947—from the study of classical antiquity to the broader topic of the rise and fall of civilizations. By the 1930s, however, a very different perspective on Thucydides was making its appearance in Germany, where Heinrich Weinstock inferred from Thucydides' text that the Greeks' success derived from the focus of all their activities on the state, a model for the ideology of the Third Reich, and Felix Wasserman construed Pericles' funeral speech as a call for the utter subordination of the individual to a state guided by an absolute leader: a Führer.

Modern advocates for democracy have, for their part, suggested that Thucydides' motive in telling the story of the Peloponnesian War was to make clear how imperialism, a bad thing, inhibited the Athenians from making the world safe for democracy, the very best of all good things. In 1919 American president Woodrow Wilson reread Thucydides' *History* on his voyage across the Atlantic en route to the Versailles Peace Conference. In 1947 United States Secretary of State George Marshall, speaking at Princeton University, declared, 'I doubt seriously whether a man can think with full wisdom and with deep convictions regarding certain of the basic international issues today who has not at least reviewed in his mind the period of the Peloponnesian War and the fall of Athens.'

Because of the Americans' periodic intervention in faraway conflicts, thinkers in the United States have been particularly preoccupied with Thucydides, whose name is perceived as lending a cloak of legitimacy to any argument. A whole book could easily be written on the use and abuse of Thucydides in America over the past 100 years. During the war in Vietnam, champions of the undertaking pointed to the insufficient support given by the Athenians to their forces in Sicily as the predictor of the ambivalent Americans' failure, while those who opposed the war insisted that Thucydides' account warned of the futility of overseas adventures in faraway and unfamiliar territory. W. Robert Connor, the former director of the National Humanities Center and the author of an extraordinarily insightful book on Thucydides, reported that he found himself connecting with Thucydides in a new way during the Vietnam War. In 2000 Lawrence Tritle, a historian at Loyola University in Los Angeles who had served in Vietnam, used parallels between the wars to explore the nature of war itself in his book *From Melos to My Lai: Violence, Culture, and Survival.*

The parallels have persisted into the 21st century. Strategy consultant Stefan Haid has compared American intervention in the Middle East with the Athenians' expedition to Sicily, attributing both to a comparable mixture of greed, fear, and the quest for glory and cautioning of the consequences of overstretched resources and ignorance of faraway lands. The Trump White House was positively obsessed with Thucydides; chief strategist Steve Bannon identified with Sparta in the Peloponnesian War, while Secretary of Defense James Mattis strongly recommended that people familiarize themselves with Thucydides' *History,* a work he himself knew well.

The notion that Thucydides' paradigm for international relations is predictive of all history has been long in the making. In 1925 British historian George Abbott explained that he had undertaken his *Thucydides: A Study in Historical Reality* in the hope that an understanding of Thucydides might be of practical use in his own day. Like Toynbee, Abbott viewed Thucydides' interpretation of the Peloponnesian War as paradigmatic. Three times, he wrote, modern Europe had been torn asunder by a conflict in essence similar to the Peloponnesian War, first by wars against France (the France of Louis XIV and the France of the revolution) and again by the First World War. 'The cause of these struggles', he concluded, 'might, after changing the names, be summed up in Thucydides' phrase: "the growth of the Athenian power which alarmed the Lacedaemonians and forced them into war."'

Nearly a century later and on the opposite side of the Atlantic Graham Allison of Harvard took up the argument for universal application in his book *Destined for War: Can America and China Escape Thucydides's Trap?* The book had everything—Harvard! Thucydides! Certainty! Doom!—and it immediately became a bestseller. My friends and relations suddenly began considering the possibility that perhaps what I do for a living isn't completely pointless after all. The Peloponnesian War, Allison argued, showed that war resulted when a rising power challenged an existing power as had happened when Sparta's supremacy in Greece was threatened by the expansion of Athens; like Abbott, Allison also collected a number of other instances of such wars, in his case a full dozen. Had not Thucydides explained that the war broke out because of the growing power of Athens and the fear it occasioned in Sparta? Thucydides' own text, however, would seem to undermine this interpretation, as those like Archidamus who were troubled by Athens's greater power did not want war. Sthenelaidas and his supporters voted for war because they were angry, not because they were afraid.

Numerous scholars have attacked Allison's arguments, contending that China's concerns are largely regional; that China is far too weak for such a conflict, given its inferior military and more limited network of alliances; that far from growing in strength China is being weakened by extensive emigration and an ageing population; and that in any case the universe of the Greek city-states is too different from the modern world for analogies to be reliable. Even had Thucydides been correct, there strikes me as something peculiar about extrapolating from the observation of a subtle reflective thinker, a man well aware of the complexity of causation, to form iron laws of history. Similar patterns would repeat themselves throughout history, Thucydides had contended, human nature being what it is; but human nature, as he knew, is not uniform. Some behaved badly during the plague, but others did not: some, he said, were unsparing in their devotion to their sick friends and made a point of visiting households where the members of the family were completely overwhelmed by the wretchedness of the situation.

The modern tendency to assume Thucydidean infallibility has led to much gross oversimplification. Because Thucydides' insights are timeless and unerring, it is often argued, we disregard them at our peril, and our failure accurately to grasp his meaning at every turn will have the direst of consequences. If, on the other hand, we can attain to a clear understanding of his text, salvation may lie ahead. These jeremiads have gone too far. Thucydides' observation that the future, given human nature, would resemble the past should not be taken to suggest facile one-to-one correspondences. As James Palmer wrote in an essay in *Foreign Policy* entitled 'Oh God, Not the Peloponnesian War Again', 'Thucydides is great, but he doesn't have to hold the same grip on IR scholars that *Harry Potter* does on millennial readers.' The value of history, wrote British philosopher of history R. G. Collingwood, 'is that it teaches us what man has done and thus what man is'. Thucydides could not have agreed more. But it does not place humanity in a straitjacket from whose confines we cannot escape; if it did, it would not be history.

References

Chapter 3: Thucydides the historian

Von Ranke's famous dictum appears in the foreword to Part I of his 1824 *Histories of the Romanic and Germanic Peoples from 1494 to 1514*.

Chapter 5: Thucydides the narrator

I refer here to G. E. M. de Sainte Croix, 'Chapter VII, The Megarian decrees', in *The Origins of the Peloponnesian War* (Ithaca, NY: Cornell University Press, 1972), 225–89.

Chapter 8: Thucydides' legacy

John Adams's letter to Jefferson of 3 February 1812 appears in Lester J. Cappon, ed., *The Adams–Jefferson Letters: The Complete Correspondence between Thomas Jefferson and Abigail and John Adams* (Chapel Hill, NC: University of North Carolina Press, 1959), 2. 295.

Leonardi Bruni's comment to Niccolo Niccoli is cited in Paul Botley, *Latin Translation in the Renaissance: The Theory and Practice of Leonardo Bruni, Giannozzo Manetti and Desiderius Erasmus* (Cambridge: Cambridge University Press, 2004), 11.

Francis Bacon's observations appear in his *Considerations Touching a Warre with Spaine*, in William Rawley, ed., *Certaine Miscellany Works of the Right Honorable, Francis Lo. Verulam, Viscount S. Alban* (London, 1629), 12–13.

Arnold's approach to Athens and his contrast between 5th-century Athens and 16th-century England is discussed in Elizabeth Potter, 'The education offered by Athens: Thucydides and the stirrings of democracy in Britain', in Katherine Harloe and Neville Morley, eds., *Thucydides and the Modern World: Reception, Reinterpretation and Influence from the Renaissance to the Present* (Cambridge: Cambridge University Press, 2012), 108–9.

May's citation in *Democracy in Europe* (London: Longman's, 1877) appears at 1. 42.

For Adams's observation see *A Defence of the Constitutions of Government of the United States of America* (1787–8, reprint New York: Da Capo Press, 1971), 181–2, 322–4.

For the remarks of Weinstock and Wassermann, see Benjamin Earley, *The Thucydidean Turn: (Re)interpreting Thucydides' Political Thought Before, During and After the Great War* (London: Bloomsbury Academic, 2020), 134–5.

Marshall's speech is reproduced in the US *Department of State Bulletin* 16, 391.

George Abbott, *Thucydides: A Study in Historical Reality* (London: Russell & Russell, 1925), v, 3–4.

Palmer's essay is at <https://foreignpolicy.com/2020/07/28/oh-god-not-the-peloponnesian-war-again/>.

Collingwood's observation appears on p. 10 of *The Idea of History* (Oxford: Clarendon, 1946; reprinted London: Lume Books, 2018).

Further reading

There are any number of excellent translations of Thucydides into English. Three editions that contain a good deal of auxiliary material are

Blanco, Walter and Jennifer Tolbert Roberts. 1998. *The Peloponnesian War: A New Translation. Backgrounds and Contexts, Interpretations*. New York: W. W. Norton.

Mynott, Jeremy. 2013. *Thucydides: The War of the Peloponnesians and the Athenians* (Cambridge Texts in the History of Political Thought). Cambridge: Cambridge University Press.

Strassler, Robert, ed. 1996. *The Landmark Thucydides: A Comprehensive Guide to the Peloponnesian War*, trans. Richard Crawley. New York: The Free Press.

With its numerous maps and essays on Greek warfare and related topics, Strassler is best for following the course of the war. Blanco & Roberts contains the portions of Xenophon's *Hellenica* that take the war's history down to its end in 404 as well as a number of essays and is best for understanding the thought of Thucydides. Mynott has an outstanding introduction, and the appendices include a very instructive collection of ancient responses to Thucydides.

There are two superb English language commentaries on Thucydides, both of them works of extraordinary erudition and utility. *The Historical Commentary on Thucydides* (often abbreviated HCT) put together over a period of years by A. W. Gomme, Antony Andrewes, and K. J. Dover was published by Oxford in several volumes from 1945 to 1981. Although it was put together in the expectation that readers would know Greek and does not translate passages it cites from Thucydides' text, it is certainly accessible to Greekless readers, who can easily find the passages in question through book and chapter references. Somewhat more user-friendly is the equally fine three-volume commentary of Simon Hornblower (Oxford University Press, 1991 to 2008), *A Commentary on Thucydides*, which translates all the Greek and has the added advantage of the author's intimate familiarity with the earlier work.

Several collections of fine essays on Thucydides have been published in recent years. Among the best are:

Balot, Ryan K., Sara Forsdyke, and Edith Foster, eds. 2017. *The Oxford Handbook of Thucydides*. Oxford and New York: Oxford University Press.

Foster, Edith and Donald Lateiner, eds. 2012. *Thucydides & Herodotus*. Oxford: Oxford University Press.

Rengakos, Antonios and Antonis Tsakmakis, eds. 2012. *Brill's Companion to Thucydides*, 2 vols. Leiden and Boston: Brill.

Rusten, Jeffrey S., ed. 2009. *Thucydides* (Oxford Readings in Classical Studies). New York: Oxford University Press.

Tsakmakis, A. and M. Tamiolaki, eds. 2013. *Thucydides Between History and Literature*. Boston and Berlin: De Gruyter.

Xenophon's *Hellenica* (*Greek Affairs*) takes up the narrative where Thucydides left off and continues all the way to 362. A convenient Penguin edition translated by Rex Warner and edited by G. L. Cawkwell was published in 1979 under the title *A History of My Times*. *The Landmark Xenophon's Hellenika* edited by Robert Strassler with a translation by John Marincola (New York: Anchor, 2010) is decked out with the customary Landmark maps and background essays.

There are numerous paperback editions of other primary sources that shed light on Thucydides' work such as Herodotus' *Histories*, Plutarch's biographies of Pericles, Nicias, and Alcibiades, the comedies of Aristophanes, and the plays of the Greek tragedians.

Useful books on the Peloponnesian War and the people who figure most prominently in it include:

Azoulay, Vincent. 2014. *Pericles of Athens*, trans. Janet Lloyd with foreword by Paul Cartledge. Princeton: Princeton University Press.

Badian, Ernst. 1993. *From Plataea to Potidaea: Studies in the History and Historiography of the Pentecontaetia*. Baltimore: The Johns Hopkins University Press.

Forde, Steven. 1989. *The Ambition to Rule: Alcibiades and the Politics of Imperialism in Thucydides*. Ithaca, NY: Cornell University Press.

Hanson, Victor D. 2011. *A War Like No Other: How the Athenians and Spartans Fought the Peloponnesian War*. New York: Random House.

Henry, Madeleine. 1995. *Prisoner of History: Aspasia of Miletus and her Biographical Tradition*. Oxford and New York: Oxford University Press.

Kagan, Donald. 2005. *The Peloponnesian War*. New York: HarperCollins.

Lendon, J. E. 2010. *Song of Wrath: The Peloponnesian War Begins*. New York: Basic Books.

Rhodes, P. J. 2011. *Alcibiades: Athenian Playboy, General and Traitor*. Barnsley: Pen and Sword.

Roberts, Jennifer T. 2017. *The Plague of War: Athens, Sparta, and the Struggle for Ancient Greece*. New York and Oxford: Oxford University Press.

Tritle, Lawrence A. 2009. *A New History of the Peloponnesian War*. Malden, Mass.: Wiley-Blackwell.

Books (entirely or in part) on Thucydides include:

Cawkwell, George. 1997. *Thucydides and the Peloponnesian War*. London and New York: Routledge.

Connor, W. R. 1984. *Thucydides*. Princeton: Princeton University Press.

Crane, Gregory. 1997. *The Ancient Simplicity: Thucydides and the Limits of Political Realism*. Berkeley and Los Angeles: University of California Press.

deRomilly, Jacqueline. 2012 (original French 1967). *The Mind of Thucydides*, trans. Elizabeth T. Rawlings, ed. Hunter R. Rawlings III and Jeffrey Rusten. Ithaca, NY: Cornell University Press.

Edmunds, Lowell. 1975. *Chance and Intelligence in Thucydides.* Cambridge, Mass.: Harvard University Press.

Foster, Edith. 2010. *Thucydides, Pericles and Periclean Imperialism.* Cambridge: Cambridge University Press.

Greenwood, Emily. 2006. *Thucydides and the Shaping of History.* London: Bloomsbury Academic.

Hunter, Virginia. 1982. *Past and Process in Herodotus and Thucydides.* Princeton: Princeton University Press.

Johnson, Laurie. *Thucydides, Hobbes, and the Interpretation of Realism.* DeKalb, Ill.: Northern Illinois University Press, 1993.

Kagan, Donald. 2009. *Thucydides: The Reinvention of History.* New York: Viking.

Kallet-Marx, Lisa. 1993. *Money, Expense, and Naval Power in Thucydides' History 1–5.24.* Berkeley: University of California Press.

Orwin, Clifford. 1994. *The Humanity of Thucydides.* Princeton: Princeton University Press.

Palmer, Michael. 1992. *Love of Glory and the Common Good: Aspects of the Political Thought of Thucydides.* Lanham, Md.: Rowman and Littlefield.

Parry, Adam. 1981. *Logos and Ergon in Thucydides.* With a new introduction by Donald Kagan. Salem, NH: Ayer.

Pelling, Christopher. 2002. *Literary Texts and the Greek Historian* (Approaching the Ancient World). London: Routledge.

Pouncey, Peter. 1980. *The Necessities of War: A Study of Thucydides' Pessimism.* New York: Columbia University Press.

Rawlings, Hunter R., III. 1981. *The Structure of Thucydides' History.* Princeton: Princeton University Press.

Rood, Tim. 1998. *Thucydides: Narrative and Explanation* (Oxford Classical Monographs). Oxford: Oxford University Press.

Stadter, P. A., ed. 1973. *The Speeches in Thucydides.* Chapel Hill, NC: University of North Carolina Press.

Westlake, H. D. 1968. *Individuals in Thucydides.* London: Cambridge University Press.

Wohl, Victoria. 2009. *Love Among the Ruins: The Erotics of Democracy in Classical Athens.* Princeton: Princeton University Press.

Woodhead, A. G. 1970. *Thucydides on the Nature of Power.* Martin Classical Lectures, 24. Cambridge, Mass.: Harvard University Press.

For the legacy of Thucydides, see:

Earley, Benjamin. 2020. *The Thucydidean Turn: (Re)interpreting Thucydides' Political Thought Before, During, and After the Great War.* London: Bloomsbury Academic.

Harloe, Katherine and Neville Morley, eds. 2012. *Thucydides and the Modern World: Reception, Reinterpretation and Influence from the Renaissance to the Present.* Cambridge: Cambridge University Press.

Lee, Christine and Neville Morley. 2014. *A Handbook to the Reception of Thucydides* (Wiley-Blackwell Handbooks to Classical Reception). Malden, Mass.: Wiley-Blackwell.

Thomas, Charlotte C. S., ed. 2019. *Power and the People: Thucydides' History and the American Founding.* Macon, Ga.: Mercer University Press.

Tritle, Lawrence A. 2000. *From Melos to My Lai: Violence, Culture, and Survival.* London: Routledge.

Index

For the benefit of digital users, indexed terms that span two pages (e.g., 52–53) may, on occasion, appear on only one of those pages.

Index

Index

125

ARISTOCRACY
A Very Short Introduction
William Doyle

This short introduction shows how ideas of aristocracy originated in ancient times, were transformed in the Middle Ages, and have only fallen apart over the last two centuries. The myths in which aristocracies have always sought to shroud themselves are stripped away, but the true sources of their enduring power are also revealed. Their outlook and behaviour affected the rest of society in innumerable and sometimes surprising ways, but perhaps most surprising was the way in which a centuries-old aristocratic hegemony crumbled away over the last two hundred years. In this *Very Short Introduction* William Doyle considers why this happened and what remains today.

www.oup.com/vsi

ARISTOTLE
A Very Short Introduction
Jonathan Barnes

The influence of Aristotle, the prince of philosophers, on the intellectual history of the West is second to none. In this *Very Short Introduction* Jonathan Barnes examines Aristotle's scientific research, his discoveries in logic, his metaphysical theories, his work in psychology, ethics, and politics, and his ideas about art and poetry, placing his teachings in their historical context.

'With compressed verve, Jonathan Barnes displays the extraordinary versatility of Aristotle, the great systematising empiricist.'

Sunday Times

AUGUSTINE
A Very Short Introduction
Henry Chadwick

The surviving bulk of Augustine's writings exceeds that of any other ancient author. Through these writings he came to influence not only his contemporaries but also the subsequent development of Western culture.

This *Very Short Introduction* traces the development of Augustine's thought, discussing his reaction to the other thinkers before him, and themes such as freedom, creation, and the Trinity.

www.oup.com/vsi

BABYLONIA
A Very Short Introduction
Trevor Bryce

The history of Ancient Babylonia in ancient Mesopotamia is epic. After playing host to three great empires, it was conquered by the Persians, entered triumphantly by Alexander the Great, and later provided the setting for the Conquerer's deathbed. Squabbled over by his heirs, Babylonia was subsequently dominated by the Parthian and Roman empires.

In this *Very Short Introduction*, Trevor Bryce takes us on a journey of more than 2,000 years across the history and civilization of ancient Babylonia. Exploring key historical events as well as the day-to-day life of an ancient Babylonian, Bryce provides a comprehensive guide to one of history's most profound civilizations.

www.oup.com/vsi

BIOGRAPHY
A Very Short Introduction
Hermione Lee

Biography is one of the most popular, best-selling, and widely-read of literary genres. But why do certain people and historical events arouse so much interest? How can biographies be compared with history and works of fiction? Does a biography need to be true? Is it acceptable to omit or conceal things? Does the biographer need to personally know the subject? Must a biographer be subjective? In this *Very Short Introduction* Hermione Lee considers the cultural and historical background of different types of biographies, looking at the factors that affect biographers and whether there are different strategies, ethics, and principles required for writing about one person compared to another. She also considers contemporary biographical publications and considers what kind of 'lives' are the most popular and in demand.

'It would be hard to think of anyone better to provide a crisp contribution to OUP's Very Short Introductions.'

Kathryn Hughes, The Guardian

BYZANTIUM
A Very Short Introduction
Peter Sarris

After surviving the fifth-century fall of the Western European
Roman Empire, the Byzantine Empire flourished as one of the
most powerful economic, cultural, and military forces in Europe
for a thousand years.

In this *Very Short Introduction* Peter Sarris introduces the reader
to the unique fusion of Roman political culture, Greek intellectual
tradition, and Christian faith that took place in the imperial capital
of Byzantium. Using examples from Byzantine architecture, art,
and literature, Sarris shows how their legacy was re-worked and
re-invented in the centuries ahead.

www.oup.com/vsi

CLASSICAL
MYTHOLOGY
A Very Short Introduction
Helen Morales

From Zeus and Europa, to Diana, Pan, and Prometheus, the myths of ancient Greece and Rome seem to exert a timeless power over us. But what do those myths represent, and why are they so enduringly fascinating? This imaginative and stimulating *Very Short Introduction* is a wide-ranging account, examining how classical myths are used and understood in both high art and popular culture, taking the reader from the temples of Crete to skyscrapers in New York, and finding classical myths in a variety of unexpected places: from Arabic poetry and Hollywood films, to psychoanalysis, the bible, and New Age spiritualism.

www.oup.com/vsi

HERODOTUS
A Very Short Introduction
Jennifer T. Roberts

Herodotus: A Very Short Introduction introduces readers to what little is known of Herodotus' life and goes on to discuss all aspects of his work, including his fascination with his origins; his travels; his view of the world in relation to boundaries and their transgressions; and his interest in seeing the world and learning about non-Greek civilizations. We also explore the recurring themes of his work, his beliefs in dreams, oracles, and omens, the prominence of women in his work, and his account of the battles of the Persian Wars.

MUHAMMAD
A Very Short Introduction
Jonathan A. C. Brown

As the founder of Islam Muhammad is one of the most influential figures in history. The furore surrounding the Satanic Verses and the Danish cartoon crisis reminded the world of the tremendous importance of the prophet of Islam, Muhammad. Learning about his life and understanding its importance, however, has always proven difficult. Our knowledge of Muhammad comes from the biography of him written by his followers, but Western historians have questioned the reliability of this story in their quest to uncover the 'historical Muhammad'. This *Very Short Introduction* provides an introduction to the major aspects of Muhammad's life and its importance, providing both the Muslim and Western historical perspectives.

'This is an excellent introduction to the life of Muhammad. Dr Brown is providing the reader with a rigorous study based on the classical Islamic tradition, yet well balanced between elements of faith and rational discussions, useful for Muslims and non Muslims alike. Very easy to read, profound and interesting to study.'

Tariq Ramadan

www.oup.com/vsi

PAUL
A Very Short Introduction
E. P. Sanders

Paul is the most powerful human personality in the history of the Church. A missionary, theologian, and religious genius, he laid down in his epistles the foundations on which later Christian theology was built.

In this highly original introduction to Paul's life and thought, E. P. Sanders, whose research on Paul has substantially influenced recent scholarship, pays equal attention to Paul's fundamental convictions and the sometimes convoluted ways in which they were worked out.

> 'Sanders' book is designed to be rounded and comprehensive and fulfils that specification magisterially and with as little technicality as one can sensibly ask.'
>
> **J. L. Houlden, Times Literary Supplement**

> 'He presents Paul, for all his inconsistencies, with great clarity and insight...The book is an apt introduction to Paul; a bold confrontation of the boldest of Christian theologians...his interpretation is eloquent for his generation and historically a clear advance.'
>
> **Church Times**

www.oup.com/vsi

ROMAN BRITAIN
A Very Short Introduction
Peter Salway

Britain was within the orbit of Graeco-Roman civilization for at least half a millenium, and for over 350 years part of the political union created by the Roman Empire that encompassed most of Europe and all the countries of the Mediterranean.

Peter Salway's *Very Short Introduction* to Roman Britain weaves together the results of archaeological investigation and historical scholarship in a rounded and highly readable account. He charts the history of Britain from the first invasion under Julius Casear to the final collapse of the Romano-British way of life in the 5th century AD.

THE ANGLO-SAXON AGE

A Very Short Introduction

John Blair

John Blair's *Very Short Introduction* to the Ango-Saxon Age covers the period from the earliest English settlements to the Norman victory in 1066.

This book introduces the reader to the political, social, religious, and cultural history of an age when so many basic aspects of modern England were formed: its language, governmental institutions, rural landscape, communications, and towns.

www.oup.com/vsi

THE HELLENISTIC AGE

A Very Short Introduction

Peter Thonemann

The three centuries which followed the conquests of Alexander are perhaps the most thrilling of all periods of ancient history. This was an age of cultural globalization: in the third century BC, a single language carried you from the Rhône to the Indus. A Celt from the lower Danube could serve in the mercenary army of a Macedonian king ruling in Egypt, and a Greek philosopher from Cyprus could compare the religions of the Brahmins and the Jews on the basis of first-hand knowledge of both. Kings from Sicily to Tajikistan struggled to meet the challenges of ruling multi-ethnic states, and Greek city-states came together under the earliest federal governments known to history. The scientists of Ptolemaic Alexandria measured the circumference of the earth, while pioneering Greek argonauts explored the Indian Ocean and the Atlantic coast of Africa.

Drawing on inscriptions, papyri, coinage, poetry, art, and archaeology, Peter Thonemann opens up the history and culture of the vast Hellenistic world, from the death of Alexander the Great (323 BC) to the final stand of Cleopatra (30 BC).

www.oup.com/vsi